DECODING PAIN WITH EXERCISES

An Overview

DR. P.V. HARI HARA SUBRAMANYAN

DR. KAMALAKANNAN.M

DR. P.G. MAHESH KUMAR

Copyright © Dr. P.V. Hari Hara Subramanyan, Dr. Kamalakannan.M and Dr. P.G. Mahesh Kumar. All Rights Reserved. This book has been self-published with all reasonable efforts taken to make the material error-free by the author. No part of this book shall be used, reproduced in any manner whatsoever without written permission from the author, except in the case of brief quotations embodied in critical articles and reviews.

The Author of this book is solely responsible and liable for its content, including but not limited to the views, representations, descriptions, statements, information, opinions, and references ["Content"]. The Content of this book shall not constitute or be construed or deemed to reflect the opinion or expression of the Publisher or Editor. Neither the Publisher nor Editor endorse or approve the Content of this book or guarantee the reliability, accuracy, or completeness of the Content published herein and do not make any representations or warranties of any kind, express or implied, including but not limited to the implied warranties of merchantability, fitness for a particular purpose. The Publisher and Editor shall not be liable whatsoever for any errors, omissions, whether such errors or omissions result from negligence, accident, or any other cause or claims for loss or damages of any kind, including without limitation, indirect or consequential loss or damage arising out of use, inability to use, or about the reliability, accuracy, or sufficiency of the information contained in this book.

Index

Foreword	*i*
Foreword	*ii*
About Authors	*iii*
Chapter Contributors	*iv*
Preface	*v*
Acknowledgements	*vii*
The Journey of Pain: An Introductory Narrative	*1*
1. *The Anatomy of Pain*	*5*
2. *The Pain Experience*	*9*
3. *Pain and Movement*	*14*
4. *Pain Across the Lifespan*	*21*
5. *Pain in Special Populations*	*34*
6. *Interdisciplinary Perspectives on Pain*	*41*
7. *Creative And Holistic Approaches*	*48*
8. *Case Studies and Clinical Applications*	*57*
9. *Future Directions in Pain Management*	*64*
10. *Conclusion*	*71*
Index (Alphabetical Order)	*75*
Abbreviations	*77*
References	*78*

Foreword

"Pain is a universal yet complex phenomenon that profoundly influences physical, emotional, and social well-being. From acute injuries to chronic conditions, its multifaceted nature demands innovative approaches. Physiotherapy emerges as a cornerstone of hope, providing evidence-based, non-invasive interventions to alleviate pain and restore function.

"Decoding Pain with Exercises – An Overview" is a transformative work that integrates cutting-edge scientific advancements with practical methodologies, making it indispensable for physiotherapists and rehabilitation professionals. By reframing pain as a multidimensional experience, this book addresses its physiological, psychological, and environmental dimensions, offering holistic strategies for effective management.

Covering a wide range of specialties—including orthopaedics, neurology, paediatrics, geriatrics, and women's health—the book delivers tailored approaches for diverse patient needs. It bridges theory and practice with insights into advanced techniques such as neurodynamic exercises and wearable technologies. Its strong emphasis on patient education empowers therapists to foster trust, dispel misconceptions, and inspire active patient participation in recovery.

The collaborative contributions of Prof. Dr. Kamalakannan M., Dr. Hariharasubramaniyan, and Dr. H. Mahesh enhance the book's depth, making it a vital resource for students, clinicians, and researchers alike. As chronic pain continues to rise, "Decoding Pain with Exercises – An Overview" inspires physiotherapists to lead the charge in delivering compassionate, effective care that transforms lives. I encourage all readers to engage deeply with this material and apply its insights to improve patient outcomes."

Prof. Dr. Prathap S.

Principal, Saveetha College of Physiotherapy

SIMATS

Foreword

Pain is an intricate and universal experience that touches every aspect of human life. It can manifest suddenly or linger for years, affecting not only physical health but also emotional stability and social interactions. As we navigate the complexities of pain, it becomes clear that effective management requires a multifaceted approach, one that is both innovative and compassionate.

"Decoding Pain with Exercises – An Overview" stands out as a pivotal contribution to the field of physiotherapy, offering a fresh perspective on pain management. This book synthesizes the latest scientific research with practical applications, making it an essential guide for physiotherapists and rehabilitation specialists. By viewing pain through a multidimensional lens, the authors provide a comprehensive framework that encompasses the physiological, psychological, and environmental factors influencing pain perception and response.

The breadth of this work is impressive, covering a diverse array of specialties such as orthopaedics, neurology, paediatrics, geriatrics, and women's health. Each chapter is thoughtfully designed to address the unique challenges faced by different patient populations, ensuring that practitioners can tailor their approaches to meet individual needs. The inclusion of advanced methodologies, including neurodynamic exercises and the integration of wearable technology, reflects a commitment to staying at the forefront of therapeutic innovation.

A standout feature of this book is its dedication to patient education. By equipping therapists with the knowledge and tools to effectively communicate with their patients, it fosters a collaborative environment that encourages active participation in the healing process. This emphasis on education not only builds trust but also empowers patients to take charge of their recovery.

The collaborative expertise of Prof. Dr. Kamalakannan M., Dr. Hariharasubramaniyan, and Prof. Dr. H. Magesh enriches this text, making it a vital resource for students, clinicians, and researchers alike. In an era where chronic pain is increasingly prevalent, "Decoding Pain with Exercises – An Overview" serves as a beacon of hope, inspiring physiotherapists to embrace their role in delivering empathetic and effective care.

I encourage all readers to immerse themselves in this invaluable resource, to explore its insights, and to implement its strategies in their practice. Together, we can redefine pain management and enhance the quality of life for those we serve.

Prof. Dr. Parthasarathy

Principal, Faculty of Physiotherapy

MAHER

About Authors

Dr. P. V. Harihara Subramanyan, MPT (Paediatrics), PhD

Dr. P. V. Harihara Subramanyan is an accomplished Associate Professor at the Faculty of Physiotherapy, Meenakshi Academy of Higher Education and Research. With nine years of teaching experience, he specializes in paediatric physiotherapy, focusing on innovative approaches to enhance motor and cognitive outcomes in children. Known for his dedication to education and research, Dr. Harihara Subramanyan is passionate about advancing paediatric rehabilitation practices and mentoring aspiring physiotherapists.

Prof. Dr. Kamalakannan M, MPT (Orthopaedics), PhD

Prof. Dr. Kamalakannan M is a distinguished academic and researcher with extensive expertise in physiotherapy. With over 11 years of teaching and research experience, and a total of 15 years in the field, he has made significant contributions to the advancement of knowledge through numerous publications in reputable journals and presentations at conferences. Renowned for his innovative approach to musculoskeletal research, Prof. Dr. Kamalakannan's work has profoundly impacted both students and professionals in the field. He currently serves as the Head of the Department of Exercise and Kinesiotherapy at Saveetha College of Physiotherapy, part of the Saveetha Institute of Medical and Technical Sciences, where he inspires the next generation of scholars through his commitment to excellence in education and research.

Dr. Mahesh Kumar P. G., MPT (Cardio Respiratory), PhD

Dr. Mahesh Kumar P. G. is a seasoned academic and clinician with over a decade of teaching experience in physiotherapy. Currently serving as a Professor at the Faculty of Physiotherapy, Meenakshi Academy of Higher Education and Research, he has dedicated his career to advancing physiotherapy education and research. His areas of expertise include innovative rehabilitation techniques, patient-centred care, and cutting-edge interventions aimed at enhancing functional outcomes. Additionally, he is an expert in cardiopulmonary rehabilitation and the management of critically ill patients in the ICU, showcasing his proficiency in optimizing recovery for this patient population. With numerous accolades in teaching and research, Dr. Mahesh is committed to mentoring the next generation of physiotherapists.

Chapter Contributors

Chapter	Title	Contributors
Chapter 1	The Anatomy of Pain	Dr. Harihara Subramanyan
Chapter 2	The Pain Experience	Dr. Kamalakannan.M
Chapter 3	Pain and Movement	Dr. Mahesh Kumar P. G
Chapter 4	Pain Across the Lifespan	Dr. Harihara Subramanyan, Dr. Kamalakannan.M
Chapter 5	Pain in Special Populations	Dr. Karthika S. R, Dr. Harihara Subramanyan
Chapter 6	Interdisciplinary Perspectives On Pain	Dr. Dhanusia, Dr. Kamalakannan.M
Chapter 7	Creative and Holistic Approaches	Dr. Suriya. N, Dr. Harihara Subramanyan
Chapter 8	Case Studies and Clinical Applications	Dr. Harihara Subramanyan, Dr. Kamalakannan.M, Dr. Mahesh Kumar P. G
Chapter 9	Future Directions in Pain Management	Dr. Harihara Subramanyan, Dr. Mohana Vidhya.M

Preface

Pain is a universal experience that transcends age, gender, and culture. It profoundly affects physical, emotional, and social well-being, yet remains one of the most complex challenges in healthcare. Decoding Pain with Exercises – An Overview is designed to address this complexity, providing a clear and practical guide to understanding and managing pain through therapeutic exercises.

Physiotherapists and rehabilitation professionals are at the forefront of pain management. We see its impact on our patients' lives and take on the responsibility of restoring their function, mobility, and quality of life. This book aims to equip professionals with evidence-based tools and strategies to assess and treat pain effectively, tailoring interventions to each patient's unique needs.

Purpose of the Book

The goal of this book is to bridge the gap between theoretical knowledge and practical application. While much literature focuses on pharmacological or surgical approaches, this resource highlights physiotherapy's essential role in managing pain through exercise. By combining scientific principles with actionable techniques, it offers a roadmap for achieving better patient outcomes.

Scope of the Book

This book takes a comprehensive approach, addressing pain across various contexts:

1. **Understanding Pain**: Explores the anatomy and physiology of pain, including the interplay between physical and psychological factors.
2. **Exercise as Therapy**: Highlights the role of movement in breaking the cycle of pain and inactivity, promoting recovery and functionality.
3. **Specialized Interventions**: Offers tailored strategies for orthopaedic, neuropathic, cardiovascular, gynaecological, and chronic pain, as well as age-specific approaches for children, adults, and the elderly.
4. **Innovations in Pain Management**: Examines new technologies like wearable devices, virtual reality, and artificial intelligence in pain care.
5. **Practical Tools**: Provides case studies, exercise protocols, and step-by-step guides for clinical application.

Target Audience

This book is intended for:

- **Physiotherapy Students**: A foundation for understanding pain management and exercise therapy.
- **Practicing Physiotherapists**: A resource for refining skills and applying innovative techniques.
- **Rehabilitation Professionals**: Practical insights for occupational therapists, sports trainers, and other specialists.

- **Researchers and Educators**: A reference for exploring new trends and teaching pain management principles.

Impact of the Book

In a time when chronic pain is a growing global health issue, Decoding Pain with Exercises – An Overview emphasizes physiotherapy's critical role in offering non-invasive, effective solutions. This book is not just a guide—it is a call to action for therapists to decode the complexities of pain, design patient-centred interventions, and transform lives.

Whether you are a student, clinician, or researcher, this book is your companion on the journey to advancing pain management. Together, we can unlock the potential of therapeutic exercise to bring relief and hope to those who need it most.

Acknowledgements

We, the authors of *Decoding Pain with Exercises – An Overview*, express our heartfelt gratitude to everyone who contributed to the successful completion of this book.

First, we thank the Almighty for providing us with strength and guidance throughout this journey. To our parents, your unconditional love and unwavering support have been our greatest source of motivation. This book is as much your achievement as it is ours.

To our families, thank you for your patience and sacrifices during the long hours spent on this work. Your encouragement and belief in us kept us going. To our friends, your support, thoughtful suggestions, and kind words have been invaluable.

We are deeply grateful to the management of our institution (MAHER and SIMATS) for their support and for fostering an environment that enabled us to embark on this endeavour. To our teachers and mentors, thank you for laying the foundation of our knowledge and inspiring us to explore and innovate.

To our students, your curiosity and enthusiasm have challenged and motivated us to think critically and strive for excellence. This book is dedicated to all learners seeking to bridge the gap between theory and practice.

We extend our gratitude to the contributors of individual chapters, whose expertise enriched this book, and to the peer reviewers and editors for their invaluable feedback and attention to detail.

Finally, we acknowledge the entire community of physiotherapists and researchers whose work inspires us every day. This book is a small contribution to a dynamic and evolving field.

To everyone who played a role in bringing this project to life—thank you.

With sincere appreciation,

The Authors

Introduction

The Journey of Pain: An Introductory Narrative

Introduction

Pain is a universal human experience, as intrinsic to our existence as breathing. It has been a companion of humanity since the dawn of time, shaping our evolution, survival, and societal structures. This chapter embarks on an in-depth exploration of the historical and scientific evolution of pain understanding, setting the stage for modern approaches in physiotherapy. By tracing the journey of pain, we gain insights into how our ancestors perceived and dealt with it, the milestones in pain research, and the revolutionary developments that have shaped contemporary pain management.

Historical Perspectives on Pain

Ancient Civilizations and Pain Perception

In ancient civilizations, pain was often interpreted through the lens of spirituality and superstition. The Egyptians, for instance, attributed pain to the displeasure of gods and sought remedies through prayers, rituals, and herbal concoctions. They also practiced trepanation, a surgical intervention involving drilling holes into the skull, believed to release evil spirits causing pain.

The Greeks and Romans, however, began to shift towards a more systematic understanding of pain. Hippocrates, often referred to as the Father of Medicine, suggested that pain was a natural phenomenon resulting from an imbalance of bodily fluids or "humours". This humoral theory dominated medical thinking for centuries. Galen, another prominent figure, advanced the understanding of pain by linking it to the nervous system, though his theories were limited by the lack of anatomical knowledge.

Medieval to Renaissance Periods

During the medieval period, pain was often seen as a test of faith or a punishment for sins. This era was marked by a significant regression in medical knowledge due to the dominance of religious dogma over scientific inquiry. However, the Renaissance sparked a renewed interest in human anatomy and physiology. Andreas Vesalius' detailed anatomical studies provided a more accurate understanding of the body's structures, laying the groundwork for future discoveries.

The Enlightenment and the Birth of Modern Pain Theory

Philosophical Shifts

The Enlightenment era brought about a paradigm shift in the understanding of pain. Philosophers like René Descartes proposed mechanistic explanations for bodily functions. Descartes' famous dualistic theory suggested that the body and mind were separate entities, with pain being a physical signal transmitted from the body to the mind via the nervous system. This was a significant departure from the mystical explanations of the past and paved the way for a more scientific approach to pain.

Advancements in Anatomy and Physiology

The 19th century witnessed groundbreaking discoveries in anatomy and physiology, furthering our understanding of pain. Scientists like Charles Bell and François Magendie conducted experiments that distinguished between sensory and motor nerves, elucidating the pathways involved in pain transmission. The discovery of specific pain receptors, or nociceptors, by Max von Frey marked a pivotal moment in pain research, highlighting the specialized nature of pain perception.

The 20th Century: A Century of Discovery

The Gate Control Theory

One of the most significant advancements in pain research came in the mid-20th century with the introduction of the Gate Control Theory by Ronald Melzack and Patrick Wall in 1965. This theory revolutionized the understanding of pain by suggesting that pain signals could be modulated by neural mechanisms within the spinal cord, acting as a "gate" that either amplifies or diminishes pain signals before they reach the brain. This concept provided a framework for understanding the complex interplay between sensory input, neural pathways, and psychological factors in pain perception.

Psychological Dimensions of Pain

The latter half of the 20th century also saw a growing recognition of the psychological dimensions of pain. Researchers like Henry Beecher observed that soldiers with severe injuries reported less pain compared to civilians with similar injuries, highlighting the role of psychological factors such as attention, emotion, and context in pain perception. This led to the development of cognitive-behavioural therapies aimed at addressing the psychological aspects of pain, complementing the physiological approaches.

Modern Approaches to Pain Management

Interdisciplinary Pain Management

The modern era of pain management is characterized by an interdisciplinary approach that integrates insights from medicine, psychology, physiotherapy, and other fields. This holistic approach recognizes that pain is a multifaceted experience influenced by biological, psychological, and social factors. Pain management now often involves a combination of pharmacological treatments, physical therapies, psychological interventions, and lifestyle modifications.

Advances in Neuroimaging and Pain Research

Technological advancements, particularly in neuroimaging, have provided unprecedented insights into the neural mechanisms of pain. Functional MRI (fMRI) and positron emission tomography (PET) scans have allowed researchers to visualize brain activity in response to pain stimuli, uncovering the complex networks involved in pain processing. These studies have revealed that pain is not just a sensory experience but also involves emotional and cognitive components, mediated by various brain regions.

The Role of Physiotherapy in Pain Management

Physiotherapy has emerged as a cornerstone of modern pain management, emphasizing the importance of movement and exercise in alleviating pain. Physiotherapists use a range of techniques, including manual therapy, therapeutic exercises, and education, to help patients manage pain, improve function, and enhance quality of life. This approach is grounded in the understanding that physical activity can modulate pain pathways, promote tissue healing, and improve psychological well-being.

Revolutionary Developments in Pain Management

Personalized Pain Management

One of the most promising developments in pain management is the move towards personalized, or precision, medicine. Advances in genetics and biomarker research have opened the possibility of tailoring pain treatments to individual patients based on their genetic makeup, pain mechanisms, and psychological profiles. This personalized approach aims to enhance treatment efficacy and minimize adverse effects.

Integrative and Complementary Therapies

The growing acceptance of integrative and complementary therapies has broadened the toolkit for pain management. Techniques such as acupuncture, mindfulness meditation, yoga, and chiropractic care are increasingly being incorporated into pain management plans. These therapies often focus on the holistic well-being of patients, addressing both the physical and emotional aspects of pain.

Technological Innovations

Technology continues to drive innovation in pain management. Wearable devices that monitor physiological parameters, virtual reality systems that provide immersive distraction during painful procedures, and neuromodulation techniques that directly alter pain pathways are just a few examples of how technology is being harnessed to improve pain management. Additionally, artificial intelligence and machine learning are being used to analyze large datasets, identify patterns, and predict treatment outcomes, further enhancing personalized pain management strategies.

The Future of Pain Management

Ongoing Research and Innovation

The journey of pain understanding is far from complete. Ongoing research continues to uncover new insights into the mechanisms of pain and develop innovative treatment approaches. The integration of interdisciplinary knowledge, technological advancements, and personalized medicine holds great promise for the future of pain management.

Shifting Paradigms

The future of pain management is likely to see a continued shift towards more holistic and patient-centred approaches. This includes not only addressing the physical aspects of pain but also considering the emotional, social, and environmental factors that influence pain perception and experience. Emphasis on patient education and self-management strategies will empower individuals to take an active role in managing their pain.

Global Health Implications

As our understanding of pain evolves, it is crucial to address the global burden of pain. Chronic pain affects millions of people worldwide, impacting their quality of life and productivity. Efforts to improve access to effective pain management, particularly in low-resource settings, are essential. This includes developing cost-effective interventions, training healthcare professionals, and raising awareness about the importance of pain management.

The journey of pain understanding has been long and complex, marked by significant milestones and revolutionary developments. From ancient superstitions to modern scientific breakthroughs, our understanding of pain has evolved dramatically. Today, pain management is a dynamic and interdisciplinary field that continues to advance, driven by ongoing research, technological innovation, and a commitment to improving patient outcomes. As we move forward, the integration of personalized medicine, holistic approaches, and global health considerations will shape the future of pain management, ensuring that individuals can lead healthier, more fulfilling lives free from the debilitating effects of pain.

1
The Anatomy of Pain

Decoding Pain: Breaking Down the Complexities of Pain Physiology, Neurobiology, and the McGill Pain Questionnaire's 20 Types of Pain

Introduction

Understanding the anatomy of pain requires an exploration of the physiological and neurobiological mechanisms that underlie pain perception. This includes examining how pain signals are generated, transmitted, and processed in the body and brain. Additionally, the McGill Pain Questionnaire (MPQ) offers a comprehensive framework for categorizing and describing pain, which is crucial for both clinical assessment and research.

Pain Physiology

Nociception: The Detection of Pain

Pain begins with nociception, the process by which specialized sensory neurons called nociceptors detect harmful or potentially harmful stimuli. Nociceptors are found in various tissues, including skin, muscles, joints, and internal organs. They respond to mechanical, thermal, and chemical stimuli, triggering an electrical signal known as an action potential.

Transmission of Pain Signals

Once activated, nociceptors transmit pain signals via peripheral nerves to the spinal cord. These signals travel along A-delta and C fibres, which differ in their conduction speeds and roles:

- **A-delta fibres** are myelinated and conduct fast, sharp, and well-localized pain (e.g., a pinprick).
- **C fibres** are unmyelinated and conduct slow, dull, and diffuse pain (e.g., aching or burning sensations).

Spinal Cord Processing

Pain signals enter the spinal cord through the dorsal horn, where they are processed and modulated. Here, pain signals can be amplified or dampened by interneurons and descending inhibitory pathways. The gate control theory of pain, proposed by Melzack and Wall, posits that a "gate" in the spinal cord modulates the transmission of pain signals to the brain. This gate can be influenced by various factors, including sensory input and psychological states.

Chapter 1 – The Anatomy of Pain

Ascending Pathways to the Brain

From the spinal cord, pain signals ascend to the brain through several pathways:

- **Spinothalamic tract**: Transmits pain and temperature signals to the thalamus, which then relays them to the primary somatosensory cortex.
- **Spinoreticular tract**: Involved in the emotional and motivational aspects of pain, projecting to the reticular formation and then to the thalamus and limbic system.
- **Spinomesencephalic tract**: Projects to the midbrain, including the periaqueductal gray (PAG), which plays a crucial role in pain modulation.

Brain Processing

In the brain, pain signals are processed in multiple regions, each contributing to different aspects of the pain experience:

- **Primary somatosensory cortex**: Responsible for the localization and intensity of pain.
- **Anterior cingulate cortex**: Involved in the emotional response to pain.
- **Insular cortex**: Integrates sensory and emotional aspects of pain.
- **Prefrontal cortex**: Associated with the cognitive evaluation of pain.
- **Limbic system**: Involved in the emotional and motivational dimensions of pain.

Neurobiology of Pain

Neurotransmitters and Pain Modulation

Pain modulation involves various neurotransmitters that either amplify or inhibit pain signals. Key neurotransmitters include:

- **Glutamate**: The primary excitatory neurotransmitter that amplifies pain signals.
- **Substance P**: Facilitates the transmission of pain signals in the spinal cord.
- **Endorphins and enkephalins**: Endogenous opioids that inhibit pain signals by binding to opioid receptors.
- **Serotonin and norepinephrine**: Involved in descending inhibitory pathways that modulate pain.

Neuroplasticity and Chronic Pain

Chronic pain is often associated with neuroplastic changes in the nervous system. Prolonged pain can lead to central sensitization, where the nervous system becomes hypersensitive to pain stimuli. This involves changes in:

- **Synaptic plasticity**: Increased excitatory synaptic transmission in the spinal cord and brain.
- **Neuronal excitability**: Enhanced responsiveness of pain neurons.
- **Glial cell activation**: Release of pro-inflammatory cytokines that amplify pain signals.

Chapter 1 – The Anatomy of Pain

Genetics and Pain

Genetic factors also play a role in pain perception and susceptibility to chronic pain. Variations in genes related to nociceptors, neurotransmitters, and pain modulation pathways can influence an individual's pain threshold and response to treatment.

The McGill Pain Questionnaire's 20 Types of Pain

The McGill Pain Questionnaire (MPQ) is a widely used tool for assessing the quality and intensity of pain. It consists of three main components: the Pain Rating Index (PRI), a numerical rating scale, and a body diagram for indicating pain locations. The PRI includes 20 categories of pain descriptors, each with several adjectives that patients can select to describe their pain.

Sensory Dimension

The sensory dimension of pain includes descriptors related to the physical characteristics of pain:

1. **Temporal**: Throbbing, pounding, pulsating
2. **Spatial**: Shooting, stabbing, lancinating
3. **Pressure**: Sharp, cutting, lacerating
4. **Thermal**: Burning, scalding, searing
5. **Phasic**: Flashing, shooting, pricking

Affective Dimension

The affective dimension of pain encompasses the emotional aspects of pain:

6. **Tension**: Tight, nagging, squeezing
7. **Fear**: Frightening, terrifying, fearful
8. **Autonomic**: Tiring, exhausting, sickening
9. **Punishment**: Cruel, vicious, punishing

Evaluative Dimension

The evaluative dimension involves an overall assessment of pain intensity and impact:

10. **Evaluative**: Annoying, troublesome, intense, unbearable

Miscellaneous Dimension

The miscellaneous dimension includes descriptors that do not fit neatly into other categories:

11. **Miscellaneous**: Spreading, radiating, and penetrating

Each of these descriptors provides a nuanced understanding of a patient's pain, helping clinicians develop more targeted and effective treatment plans.

Chapter 1 – The Anatomy of Pain

Clinical Implications

Understanding the complexities of pain physiology, neurobiology, and the MPQ's 20 types of pain has significant clinical implications. It allows for:

- **Accurate Diagnosis**: Differentiating between types of pain (e.g., nociceptive vs. neuropathic) to guide appropriate treatment.
- **Targeted Interventions**: Developing personalized treatment plans based on the specific characteristics of a patient's pain.
- **Effective Communication**: Facilitating clear communication between patients and healthcare providers about pain experiences.
- **Holistic Care**: Addressing both the physical and emotional aspects of pain for comprehensive pain management.

Decoding the complexities of pain involves an intricate understanding of its physiological and neurobiological underpinnings, as well as a sophisticated approach to pain assessment through tools like the McGill Pain Questionnaire. By comprehensively exploring these dimensions, healthcare professionals can enhance their ability to diagnose, treat, and manage pain, ultimately improving patient outcomes and quality of life.

2
The Pain Experience

Understanding Subjective Pain Perception and Its Impact on Patients' Lives

Introduction

Pain is inherently subjective, shaped by individual experiences, emotions, and contexts. Understanding the subjective nature of pain is crucial for effective pain management and patient care. This chapter delves into the nuances of pain perception, the factors influencing it, and its profound impact on patients' lives.

Subjective Nature of Pain

The Individual Experience of Pain

Pain is a personal and unique experience, varying widely from person to person. Factors that contribute to the subjective nature of pain include:

- **Genetics**: Genetic differences influence pain sensitivity and susceptibility to chronic pain.
- **Psychological State**: Emotions, stress, and mental health significantly affect pain perception.
- **Cultural and Social Context**: Cultural beliefs and social support systems shape how individuals perceive and express pain.
- **Previous Experiences**: Past pain experiences can alter an individual's pain threshold and coping strategies.

Pain Threshold and Tolerance

Pain threshold refers to the minimum intensity of a stimulus that is perceived as painful, while pain tolerance is the maximum intensity of pain an individual can endure. These thresholds are influenced by:

- **Biological Factors**: Genetic makeup, age, and gender.
- **Psychological Factors**: Anxiety, depression, and cognitive biases.
- **Environmental Factors**: Context and social environment.

Psychological Dimensions of Pain

Emotional and Cognitive Influences

Pain is not merely a sensory experience but also has significant emotional and cognitive components. Key psychological factors influencing pain include:

- **Anxiety and Fear**: Heightened anxiety can amplify pain perception, creating a vicious cycle of pain and distress.
- **Depression**: Chronic pain is often associated with depression, which can exacerbate pain intensity and hinder recovery.
- **Attention and Distraction**: Focusing on pain tends to increase its intensity, while distraction techniques can help reduce pain perception.
- **Catastrophizing**: Negative thought patterns, such as expecting the worst, can increase pain intensity and lead to poorer outcomes.

Pain Coping Mechanisms

Individuals adopt various coping mechanisms to manage pain, including:

- **Active Coping**: Engaging in activities and problem-solving strategies to manage pain (e.g., exercise, seeking social support).
- **Passive Coping**: Avoiding activities and relying on rest and medication (e.g., bed rest, painkillers).
- **Cognitive Coping**: Using mental strategies to alter pain perception (e.g., positive thinking, relaxation techniques).

Impact of Pain on Mental Health

Chronic pain can have a profound impact on mental health, leading to conditions such as:

- **Anxiety Disorders**: Chronic pain can trigger or exacerbate anxiety disorders, including generalized anxiety disorder and panic disorder.
- **Depressive Disorders**: Persistent pain is a major risk factor for developing major depressive disorder.
- **Sleep Disorders**: Pain often disrupts sleep, leading to insomnia and further exacerbating pain and emotional distress.

Sociocultural Influences on Pain

Cultural Beliefs and Pain Expression

Cultural beliefs play a crucial role in shaping pain perception and expression. Different cultures have varying attitudes towards pain and its management, influencing how individuals report and cope with pain.

Chapter 2 – The Pain Experience

For instance:

- **Stoicism vs. Expressiveness**: Some cultures value stoicism and endurance, while others encourage expressiveness and seeking help.
- **Traditional Remedies**: Cultural practices often include traditional remedies and alternative therapies for pain management.

Social Support and Pain Management

Social support systems, including family, friends, and healthcare providers, significantly impact pain experiences. Positive social support can:

- **Enhance Coping**: Provide emotional and practical assistance, improving pain management.
- **Reduce Stress**: Alleviate stress and anxiety associated with pain, contributing to better outcomes.
- **Encourage Adherence**: Promote adherence to treatment plans and healthier behaviours.

The Impact of Pain on Daily Life

Functional Impairment

Pain often leads to functional impairment, affecting daily activities and overall quality of life. Common areas of impact include:

- **Mobility**: Pain can limit physical movement and participation in activities.
- **Work and Productivity**: Chronic pain can lead to absenteeism, reduced productivity, and disability.
- **Social Interactions**: Pain may hinder social engagement and lead to isolation.

Emotional and Psychological Well-being

The emotional toll of pain can be substantial, affecting overall well-being. Pain can lead to:

- **Reduced Quality of Life**: Chronic pain significantly diminishes quality of life, leading to a sense of hopelessness and despair.
- **Emotional Distress**: Persistent pain can cause emotional turmoil, including feelings of frustration, anger, and helplessness.
- **Impact on Relationships**: Pain can strain relationships with family, friends, and partners, leading to social withdrawal and loneliness.

Assessing Subjective Pain

Pain Assessment Tools

Accurately assessing subjective pain is essential for effective pain management. Common assessment tools include:

- **Visual Analog Scale (VAS)**: A continuous scale for patients to rate their pain intensity.
- **Numeric Rating Scale (NRS)**: A numerical scale (0-10) for pain intensity.
- **McGill Pain Questionnaire (MPQ)**: A comprehensive tool that assesses sensory, affective, and evaluative dimensions of pain.
- **Brief Pain Inventory (BPI)**: Measures pain severity and its impact on daily activities.

Patient-Centered Approach

A patient-centred approach to pain assessment involves:

- **Active Listening**: Allowing patients to express their pain experiences without judgment.
- **Holistic Assessment**: Considering physical, emotional, and social aspects of pain.
- **Individualized Care**: Tailoring pain management strategies to the unique needs and preferences of each patient.

Pain Management Strategies

Pharmacological Interventions

Pharmacological treatments remain a cornerstone of pain management. Commonly used medications include:

- **Nonsteroidal Anti-inflammatory Drugs (NSAIDs)**: Reduce inflammation and alleviate mild to moderate pain.
- **Opioids**: Effective for severe pain but associated with risks of dependence and side effects.
- **Antidepressants and Anticonvulsants**: Used for neuropathic pain and chronic pain conditions.

Non-Pharmacological Interventions

Non-pharmacological approaches are essential for comprehensive pain management. These include:

- **Physical Therapy**: Exercises, manual therapy, and modalities to improve function and reduce pain.
- **Psychological Therapies**: Cognitive-behavioural therapy (CBT), mindfulness, and relaxation techniques to address the emotional aspects of pain.
- **Complementary Therapies**: Acupuncture, massage, and chiropractic care to provide additional relief.

Chapter 2 – The Pain Experience

Integrative Pain Management

An integrative approach combines pharmacological and non-pharmacological interventions, focusing on the whole person rather than just the pain. Key components include:

- **Multidisciplinary Teams**: Collaboration among healthcare professionals from various disciplines to provide comprehensive care.
- **Patient Education**: Empowering patients with knowledge and skills to manage their pain effectively.
- **Lifestyle Modifications**: Encouraging healthy behaviours, such as regular exercise, balanced nutrition, and stress management.

Understanding the subjective nature of pain and its impact on patients' lives is crucial for effective pain management. By acknowledging the individual experience of pain, addressing psychological and sociocultural influences, and employing a holistic approach to care, healthcare professionals can better support patients in managing their pain and improving their quality of life. The journey of pain is multifaceted, but with compassion, knowledge, and innovation, we can navigate it more effectively and help patients find relief and resilience.

3
Pain and Movement

The Kinetics of Pain: How Movement and Biomechanics Influence Pain and Recovery

Introduction

Movement and biomechanics are fundamental to understanding pain and its management. The kinetic chain, encompassing bones, muscles, tendons, and ligaments, plays a critical role in how pain is experienced and mitigated. This chapter delves into the intricate relationship between movement, biomechanics, and pain, exploring how movement patterns influence pain perception, the role of abnormal biomechanics in pain development, and the therapeutic strategies employed in physiotherapy to optimize recovery.

The Biomechanics of Pain

Understanding Biomechanics

Biomechanics involves the study of the mechanical laws relating to the movement or structure of living organisms. It encompasses:

- **Kinematics**: The study of motion without considering the forces that cause it.
- **Kinetics**: The study of the forces that cause motion, including internal forces (muscle contractions) and external forces (gravity, friction).

Role of Biomechanics in Pain Development

Abnormal biomechanics can contribute to the development and persistence of pain. Factors include:

- **Malalignment**: Misalignment of joints can lead to abnormal stress distribution, causing pain and degeneration.
- **Muscle Imbalance**: Disproportionate strength or flexibility in opposing muscle groups can lead to compensatory movements and pain.
- **Altered Movement Patterns**: Changes in gait or movement due to injury can perpetuate pain and dysfunction.

Chapter 3 – Pain and Movement

Biomechanical Assessments in Physiotherapy

Physiotherapists utilize various biomechanical assessments to diagnose and treat pain:

- **Gait Analysis**: Evaluating walking patterns to identify abnormalities contributing to pain.
- **Movement Screening**: Assessing functional movements to detect imbalances or compensations.
- **Postural Assessment**: Analyzing body alignment to identify sources of pain.

Example: Lower Back Pain and Biomechanics

Lower back pain often involves biomechanical factors such as:

- **Lumbar Lordosis**: Excessive curvature of the lower spine can cause muscle strain and disc problems.
- **Pelvic Tilt**: Anterior or posterior pelvic tilt can alter lumbar mechanics, leading to pain.
- **Core Stability**: Weakness in core muscles can result in poor spinal support and increased strain on the lower back.

Kinetics of Pain and Recovery

The Role of Kinetics in Pain

Kinetics focuses on the forces that cause motion, crucial for understanding pain mechanisms:

- **Muscle Forces**: Imbalances or weakness can lead to overuse and pain.
- **Joint Forces**: Abnormal loading patterns can cause joint degeneration and pain.
- **Tissue Stress**: Excessive or repetitive stress on tissues can lead to microtrauma and pain.

Therapeutic Kinetics in Physiotherapy

Physiotherapists use kinetic principles to design rehabilitation programs:

- **Strengthening Exercises**: Targeting weak muscles to restore balance and reduce pain.
- **Stabilization Exercises**: Enhancing core stability to support joints and prevent pain.
- **Manual Therapy**: Techniques such as joint mobilization and soft tissue manipulation to alleviate pain and restore normal movement.

Example: Knee Pain and Kinetics

Knee pain, particularly in conditions like patellofemoral pain syndrome, involves kinetic factors:

- **Quadriceps Strength**: Weakness can lead to altered patellar tracking and pain.
- **Hip Abductor Strength**: Insufficient strength can cause increased medial collapse of the knee, contributing to pain.
- **Foot Mechanics**: Overpronation or supination can affect knee alignment and increase pain.

Movement Patterns and Pain

Impact of Movement Patterns on Pain

Movement patterns, both habitual and compensatory, significantly influence pain:

- **Repetitive Movements**: Overuse injuries result from repetitive stress on tissues without adequate recovery.
- **Compensatory Movements**: Altered movement patterns due to pain or injury can lead to secondary pain conditions.

Identifying and Correcting Abnormal Movement Patterns

Physiotherapists assess and correct abnormal movement patterns to alleviate pain:

- **Functional Movement Screening**: Identifying dysfunctional movements that contribute to pain.
- **Motor Control Training**: Enhancing coordination and control to promote efficient movement.
- **Neuromuscular Re-education**: Retraining the nervous system to adopt healthy movement patterns.

Example: Shoulder Pain and Movement Patterns

Shoulder pain, such as in rotator cuff tendinopathy, is often influenced by movement patterns:

- Scapular Dyskinesis: Abnormal scapular movement can lead to impingement and pain.
- Poor Posture: Forward head and rounded shoulders can exacerbate shoulder pain.
- Overhead Activities: Repetitive overhead movements can cause overuse injuries and pain.

Rehabilitation Strategies in Physiotherapy

Biomechanical Correction and Pain Relief

Physiotherapists employ various strategies to correct biomechanics and alleviate pain:

- **Exercise Prescription**: Tailoring exercises to address specific biomechanical issues.
- **Manual Therapy**: Techniques to improve joint and soft tissue function.
- **Education**: Teaching patients about proper movement patterns and ergonomics.

Example: Hip Pain and Rehabilitation

Hip pain, such as in osteoarthritis, requires a comprehensive approach:

- **Strengthening Exercises**: Focusing on gluteal and hip flexor muscles to support the hip joint.
- **Mobility Exercises**: Enhancing hip range of motion to reduce stiffness and pain.
- **Gait Training**: Improving walking patterns to reduce stress on the hip joint.

Chapter 3 – Pain and Movement

Optimizing Recovery Through Movement

Movement is essential for recovery, promoting tissue healing and reducing pain:

- **Early Mobilization**: Encouraging movement soon after injury to prevent stiffness and promote circulation.
- **Progressive Loading**: Gradually increasing exercise intensity to strengthen tissues and prevent re-injury.
- **Pain Management Techniques**: Using modalities such as heat, cold, and electrical stimulation to alleviate pain and facilitate movement.

The interplay between movement, biomechanics, and pain is complex but crucial for effective pain management and recovery. By understanding the kinetics of pain and employing biomechanical assessments and interventions, physiotherapists can help patients achieve optimal function and pain relief. Through targeted exercise programs, manual therapy, and patient education, the goal is to correct abnormal movement patterns, enhance strength and stability, and ultimately improve the quality of life for those suffering from pain.

Movement as Medicine: The Role of Therapeutic Exercise in Alleviating Different Types of Pain

Introduction

Therapeutic exercise is a cornerstone of physiotherapy, offering a potent and non-invasive means of managing pain. This chapter explores the role of therapeutic exercise in alleviating various types of pain, from acute to chronic conditions. We will examine the physiological mechanisms through which exercise exerts its analgesic effects, discuss different types of therapeutic exercises, and provide evidence-based examples of exercise interventions for specific pain conditions.

Physiological Mechanisms of Exercise-Induced Pain Relief

Endogenous Opioid Release

Exercise triggers the release of endogenous opioids, such as endorphins and enkephalins, which bind to opioid receptors in the brain and spinal cord, reducing pain perception. This natural pain relief mechanism is often referred to as the "runner's high."

Anti-Inflammatory Effects

Regular physical activity has anti-inflammatory effects, reducing levels of pro-inflammatory cytokines and increasing anti-inflammatory mediators. This can alleviate pain in conditions characterized by inflammation, such as rheumatoid arthritis and tendinitis.

Chapter 3 – Pain and Movement

Neuromodulation

Exercise can modulate pain pathways through neuroplastic changes in the central nervous system. This includes enhanced inhibitory control over pain signals and increased production of neurotransmitters such as serotonin and norepinephrine, which play a role in pain modulation.

Improved Tissue Health

Therapeutic exercise promotes tissue healing by enhancing blood flow, delivering oxygen and nutrients to tissues, and facilitating the removal of metabolic waste products. This is crucial for the repair and regeneration of injured tissues.

Types of Therapeutic Exercises

Aerobic Exercise

Aerobic exercise, such as walking, cycling, and swimming, improves cardiovascular fitness and overall well-being. It is effective in reducing pain in conditions such as fibromyalgia, chronic low back pain, and osteoarthritis.

Strength Training

Strength training involves resistance exercises to build muscle mass and strength. This type of exercise is beneficial for managing pain related to musculoskeletal conditions, such as knee osteoarthritis and lower back pain, by enhancing joint stability and reducing the load on painful structures.

Flexibility and Stretching Exercises

Flexibility exercises, including static and dynamic stretching, improve range of motion and reduce muscle stiffness. These exercises are particularly useful for conditions like plantar fasciitis, neck pain, and shoulder impingement.

Balance and Proprioception Training

Balance exercises improve coordination and stability, reducing the risk of falls and injuries. Proprioception training, which enhances the body's awareness of its position in space, is crucial for rehabilitation after joint injuries, such as ankle sprains.

Mind-Body Exercises

Mind-body exercises, such as yoga and tai chi, combine physical movement with mental focus and relaxation techniques. These exercises are effective in reducing pain and improving function in conditions like chronic low back pain, osteoarthritis, and fibromyalgia.

Chapter 3 – Pain and Movement

Evidence-Based Examples of Exercise Interventions

Chronic Low Back Pain

Chronic low back pain is a prevalent condition that significantly impacts daily life. Evidence-based exercise interventions include:

- **Core Stabilization Exercises**: Strengthening the core muscles to support the spine and reduce pain.
- **McKenzie Method**: A series of exercises focusing on spinal extension to alleviate pain and improve function.
- **Aerobic Exercise**: Walking or cycling to enhance overall fitness and reduce pain perception.

Osteoarthritis

Osteoarthritis is a degenerative joint disease commonly affecting the knees and hips. Effective exercise interventions include:

- **Strength Training**: Quadriceps strengthening exercises to improve knee stability and reduce pain.
- **Aquatic Exercise**: Low-impact exercises in water to reduce joint stress and improve mobility.
- **Range of Motion Exercises**: Stretching and flexibility exercises to maintain joint function.

Fibromyalgia

Fibromyalgia is characterized by widespread musculoskeletal pain and fatigue. Therapeutic exercise plays a key role in management:

- **Aerobic Exercise**: Low to moderate-intensity aerobic activities, such as walking or swimming, to reduce pain and improve quality of life.
- **Strength Training**: Gradual resistance training to increase muscle strength and reduce pain.
- **Mind-Body Exercises**: Yoga and tai chi to enhance relaxation, reduce stress, and alleviate pain.

Shoulder Impingement Syndrome

Shoulder impingement involves compression of the rotator cuff tendons and bursa in the shoulder. Exercise interventions include:

- **Scapular Stabilization Exercises**: Strengthening the muscles that control scapular movement to improve shoulder mechanics.
- **Rotator Cuff Strengthening**: Targeted exercises to strengthen the rotator cuff muscles and reduce impingement.
- **Stretching Exercises**: Improving flexibility of the shoulder joint to alleviate pain and restore function.

Plantar Fasciitis

Plantar fasciitis is a common cause of heel pain. Effective exercise interventions include:

- **Calf Stretching**: Stretching the calf muscles to reduce tension on the plantar fascia.
- **Foot Strengthening Exercises**: Strengthening the intrinsic foot muscles to provide better arch support.
- **Rolling Exercises**: Using a foam roller or ball to massage the plantar fascia and reduce pain.

Integrating Therapeutic Exercise into Pain Management

Assessment and Individualization

A thorough assessment is essential to tailor exercise programs to individual needs. This includes evaluating the type and intensity of pain, functional limitations, and patient goals. Personalized exercise prescriptions ensure that interventions are safe, effective, and aligned with patient preferences.

Progressive Loading and Monitoring

Gradual progression in exercise intensity and volume is crucial to avoid exacerbating pain and to promote tissue adaptation. Regular monitoring and adjustment of the exercise program based on patient feedback and progress are key to successful pain management.

Education and Empowerment

Educating patients about the benefits of therapeutic exercise and empowering them to take an active role in their pain management is vital. This includes teaching proper exercise techniques, addressing barriers to exercise, and fostering a positive mindset towards physical activity.

Multidisciplinary Approach

Integrating therapeutic exercise into a multidisciplinary pain management plan enhances outcomes. Collaboration with other healthcare professionals, such as physicians, psychologists, and occupational therapists, ensures a comprehensive approach to pain management.

Therapeutic exercise is a powerful tool in the management of pain, offering numerous physiological benefits and improving patients' quality of life. By understanding the mechanisms through which exercise alleviates pain and implementing evidence-based exercise interventions, physiotherapists can effectively address various pain conditions. Movement, when prescribed appropriately, truly serves as medicine, promoting recovery, enhancing function, and empowering patients to live healthier, pain-free lives.

4
Pain Across the Lifespan

Pain in Childhood: Addressing Paediatric Pain with Innovative Exercise Solutions Introduction

Childhood pain, whether acute or chronic, can significantly impact a child's physical and emotional well-being. Understanding and addressing paediatric pain requires a unique approach that considers the developmental stages and specific needs of children. This chapter explores innovative exercise solutions tailored for paediatric pain management, emphasizing the role of physiotherapy in alleviating pain and promoting healthy development.

Understanding Paediatric Pain

Types of Paediatric Pain

Paediatric pain can be categorized into several types:

- **Acute Pain**: Often results from injury, surgery, or illness, and typically resolves as the underlying condition heals.
- **Chronic Pain**: Persists for longer periods, often without a clear cause, and can affect a child's daily activities and quality of life.
- **Recurrent Pain**: Pain that occurs intermittently, such as headaches or abdominal pain.

Common Causes of Paediatric Pain

Several conditions can cause pain in children:

- **Injuries**: Falls, fractures, and sprains are common in active children.
- **Medical Conditions**: Conditions such as juvenile idiopathic arthritis (JIA), sickle cell disease, and growing pains.
- **Post-Surgical Pain**: Pain following surgical procedures.

Physiological and Psychological Aspects of Paediatric Pain

Children experience pain differently than adults due to developmental differences:

- **Nervous System Development**: The immature nervous system can affect pain perception and response.
- **Emotional and Psychological Factors**: Anxiety, fear, and stress can amplify pain experiences in children.

Innovative Exercise Solutions for Paediatric Pain

Play-Based Therapy

Integrating play into exercise routines makes therapy enjoyable and engaging for children:

- **Obstacle Courses**: Using soft play equipment to create obstacle courses that improve strength, coordination, and flexibility.
- **Therapeutic Games**: Games that incorporate movement, such as Simon Says or relay races, to promote physical activity and pain relief.

Aquatic Therapy

Aquatic therapy leverages the properties of water to create a supportive and low-impact environment:

- **Buoyancy**: Reduces weight-bearing stress on joints and muscles, making it easier for children to move.
- **Hydrostatic Pressure**: Provides gentle resistance and supports circulation, reducing pain and inflammation.

Example: Managing Juvenile Idiopathic Arthritis

For children with JIA, exercise is crucial in maintaining joint mobility and reducing pain:

- Range of Motion Exercises: Gentle stretching to maintain flexibility and prevent contractures.
- Strengthening Exercises: Low-resistance exercises using bands or light weights to improve muscle strength around affected joints.
- Swimming: A full-body exercise that enhances cardiovascular fitness and joint mobility without excessive stress.

Virtual Reality (VR) Therapy

VR therapy offers immersive and interactive experiences that distract from pain and encourage movement:

- **Interactive Games**: VR games that require physical movement, such as boxing or dancing, to engage children in therapeutic activities.
- **Pain Distraction**: VR environments can distract children from their pain, making therapy sessions more enjoyable.

Example: Post-Surgical Pain Management

VR therapy can be particularly beneficial for managing post-surgical pain:

- **Pain Distraction**: Engaging VR experiences can divert attention away from pain, reducing the perception of discomfort.

Chapter 4 – Pain Across the Lifespan

- **Motivating Movement**: Interactive VR games encourage children to move, promoting recovery and preventing stiffness.

Physiotherapy Techniques for Paediatric Pain

Manual Therapy

Physiotherapists use gentle manual techniques to alleviate pain and improve function:

- **Massage**: Gentle massage can relieve muscle tension and reduce pain.
- **Joint Mobilization**: Techniques to improve joint mobility and reduce stiffness.

Electrotherapy

Non-invasive electrotherapy modalities can provide pain relief for children:

- **Transcutaneous Electrical Nerve Stimulation (TENS)**: Delivers low-voltage electrical currents to reduce pain perception.
- **Ultrasound Therapy**: Uses sound waves to promote tissue healing and reduce pain.

Exercise Programs

Tailored exercise programs are essential for managing paediatric pain:

- **Warm-Up and Cool-Down**: Essential components to prepare the body for exercise and prevent injury.
- **Aerobic Exercise**: Activities such as cycling, swimming, or brisk walking to improve cardiovascular health and reduce pain.
- **Strength Training**: Age-appropriate resistance exercises to build muscle strength and support joint health.

Example: Managing Growing Pains

Growing pains are common in children, typically affecting the legs:

- **Stretching Exercises**: Gentle stretching of the quadriceps, hamstrings, and calf muscles can alleviate discomfort.
- **Strengthening Exercises**: Strengthening the lower limb muscles to provide better support and reduce pain.
- **Warm Baths**: Soaking in a warm bath before bedtime can help relax muscles and reduce pain.

Parental Involvement and Education

Importance of Parental Support

Parents play a crucial role in managing their child's pain:

- **Providing Comfort**: Offering emotional support and reassurance to reduce anxiety and stress.
- **Encouraging Participation**: Motivating children to engage in exercise and therapy sessions.

Education and Resources for Parents

Educating parents about pain management strategies is vital:

- **Home Exercise Programs**: Teaching parents simple exercises that can be performed at home to support ongoing pain management.
- **Pain Management Techniques**: Providing information on techniques such as heat or cold therapy, relaxation exercises, and proper pain medication use.

Conclusion

Addressing paediatric pain requires a comprehensive approach that combines innovative exercise solutions with physiotherapy techniques. By understanding the unique needs of children and incorporating play-based therapy, aquatic therapy, VR therapy, and tailored exercise programs, physiotherapists can effectively manage pain and promote healthy development. Parental involvement and education are essential components, ensuring that children receive the support they need to overcome pain and thrive.

Pain in Adolescence: Navigating Growth-Related Pains and Sports Injuries in Teens

Introduction

Adolescence is a period of rapid growth and physical development, often accompanied by pain related to growth spurts and sports activities. Addressing pain in adolescents requires a tailored approach that considers the unique physiological and psychological aspects of this developmental stage. This chapter explores strategies for managing growth-related pains and sports injuries in teens, highlighting the role of physiotherapy in promoting recovery and preventing future injuries.

Chapter 4 – Pain Across the Lifespan

Understanding Adolescent Pain

Types of Adolescent Pain

Adolescents may experience various types of pain:

- **Growth-Related Pains**: Commonly known as growing pains, these are often felt in the legs and are associated with rapid growth periods.
- **Sports Injuries**: Injuries resulting from participation in sports and physical activities, such as sprains, strains, and overuse injuries.
- **Chronic Pain Conditions**: Conditions such as juvenile idiopathic arthritis or scoliosis that may persist into adolescence.

Physiological and Psychological Aspects of Adolescent Pain

Adolescents experience pain differently due to ongoing development:

- **Rapid Growth**: Growth spurts can cause imbalances in muscle strength and flexibility, leading to pain.
- **Hormonal Changes**: Hormonal fluctuations can affect pain perception and response.
- **Psychological Factors**: Stress, anxiety, and peer pressure can influence pain experiences and coping strategies.

Managing Growth-Related Pains

Understanding Growth-Related Pains

Growth-related pains typically occur in the legs, particularly the thighs, calves, and behind the knees. They often arise during periods of rapid growth and are more common in the evening or at night.

Exercise Solutions for Growth-Related Pains

Stretching and Flexibility Exercises

Stretching exercises help alleviate muscle tightness and discomfort associated with growth-related pains:

- **Quadriceps Stretch**: Stretching the front thigh muscles to reduce tension.
- **Hamstring Stretch**: Stretching the back thigh muscles to improve flexibility.
- **Calf Stretch**: Stretching the calf muscles to reduce tightness and pain.

Strengthening Exercises

Strengthening exercises can support muscle balance and reduce pain:

- **Leg Lifts**: Strengthening the quadriceps and hip flexors.
- **Calf Raises**: Building strength in the calf muscles to support lower leg function.
- **Core Strengthening**: Enhancing core stability to improve overall body mechanics.

Activity Modification and Rest

Adjusting activity levels and ensuring adequate rest can help manage growth-related pains:

- **Limiting High-Impact Activities**: Reducing activities that place excessive stress on growing bones and muscles.
- **Encouraging Low-Impact Activities**: Promoting activities such as swimming or cycling that are easier on the joints.

Example: Managing Osgood-Schlatter Disease

Osgood-Schlatter disease is a common cause of knee pain in adolescents:

- **Quadriceps Stretching**: Regular stretching of the quadriceps to reduce tension on the patellar tendon.
- **Strengthening Exercises**: Building strength in the quadriceps and hamstrings to support the knee joint.
- **Activity Modification**: Reducing activities that exacerbate pain, such as jumping or running, and incorporating low-impact exercises.

Managing Sports Injuries in Adolescents

Common Sports Injuries

Adolescents are prone to various sports injuries, including:

- **Sprains and Strains**: Injuries to ligaments and muscles caused by overstretching or excessive force.
- **Overuse Injuries**: Conditions such as tendinitis or stress fractures resulting from repetitive stress on tissues.
- **Fractures and Dislocations**: More severe injuries requiring immediate medical attention and rehabilitation.

Chapter 4 – Pain Across the Lifespan

Physiotherapy Interventions for Sports Injuries

Acute Injury Management

Initial management of acute sports injuries involves the RICE protocol:

- **Rest**: Avoiding activities that aggravate the injury.
- **Ice**: Applying ice to reduce swelling and pain.
- **Compression**: Using bandages or wraps to minimize swelling.
- **Elevation**: Elevating the injured limb to reduce swelling.

Rehabilitation and Exercise Programs

Rehabilitation programs are tailored to the specific injury and focus on restoring function and preventing recurrence:

- **Range of Motion Exercises**: Gentle movements to restore flexibility and prevent stiffness.
- **Strengthening Exercises**: Gradual progression of exercises to rebuild muscle strength and support the injured area.
- **Proprioception Training**: Exercises to improve balance and coordination, reducing the risk of re-injury.

Example: Managing Ankle Sprains

Ankle sprains are common in adolescents participating in sports:

- **Initial Management**: Applying the RICE protocol to reduce pain and swelling.
- **Range of Motion Exercises**: Gentle ankle circles and toe movements to restore flexibility.
- **Strengthening Exercises**: Calf raises and resistance band exercises to rebuild ankle strength.
- **Proprioception Training**: Balance exercises on a wobble board to improve stability and prevent future sprains.

Preventing Injuries and Promoting Healthy Habits

Importance of Warm-Up and Cool-Down

Proper warm-up and cool-down routines are essential for injury prevention:

- **Warm-Up**: Dynamic stretching and light aerobic exercises to prepare the body for physical activity.
- **Cool-Down**: Gentle stretching and low-intensity exercises to gradually reduce heart rate and prevent muscle stiffness.

Chapter 4 – Pain Across the Lifespan

Educating Adolescents on Injury Prevention

Providing adolescents with knowledge about injury prevention and healthy habits is crucial:

- **Proper Technique**: Teaching correct techniques for sports and exercises to reduce the risk of injury.
- **Equipment Use**: Emphasizing the importance of using appropriate protective gear and equipment.
- **Balanced Training**: Encouraging a balanced approach to training that includes rest days and cross-training to prevent overuse injuries.

Conclusion

Managing pain in adolescence requires a comprehensive approach that addresses the unique challenges of growth-related pains and sports injuries. Through tailored exercise solutions, physiotherapy interventions, and education on injury prevention, physiotherapists can help adolescents navigate this critical developmental stage with reduced pain and enhanced physical well-being. By promoting healthy habits and providing ongoing support, adolescents can achieve their full potential in sports and daily activities.

Pain in Adulthood: Coping with Chronic Pain and Lifestyle-Related Issues

Introduction

Adulthood presents various challenges related to chronic pain and lifestyle factors that can impact physical and emotional well-being. Managing pain in adults requires a multifaceted approach that considers the complexities of adult life, including work-related stress, sedentary lifestyles, and chronic health conditions. This chapter explores strategies for coping with chronic pain and addressing lifestyle-related issues, emphasizing the role of physiotherapy in promoting long-term pain relief and improved quality of life.

Understanding Adult Pain

Types of Adult Pain

Adults may experience different types of pain, including:

- Chronic Pain: Persistent pain lasting longer than three months, often without a clear cause.
- Acute Pain: Short-term pain resulting from injury, surgery, or illness.
- Referred Pain: Pain perceived in areas other than the actual source, often related to issues with internal organs or the spine.

Chapter 4 – Pain Across the Lifespan

Common Causes of Adult Pain

Several factors can contribute to pain in adulthood:

- **Work-Related Stress**: Physical and emotional stress from demanding jobs or poor ergonomics.
- **Sedentary Lifestyles**: Prolonged sitting and lack of physical activity leading to musculoskeletal issues.
- **Chronic Health Conditions**: Conditions such as arthritis, fibromyalgia, and diabetes that can cause persistent pain.

Physiological and Psychological Aspects of Adult Pain

Pain in adulthood is influenced by both physiological and psychological factors:

- **Physical Changes**: Age-related changes in the body, such as decreased muscle mass and joint degeneration.
- **Emotional Stress**: Stress, anxiety, and depression can amplify pain perception and impact coping mechanisms.

Coping with Chronic Pain

Understanding Chronic Pain

Chronic pain is complex and multifaceted, requiring a holistic approach to management:

- **Neuropathic Pain**: Pain caused by nerve damage or dysfunction.
- **Nociceptive Pain**: Pain resulting from tissue injury or inflammation.
- **Mixed Pain**: A combination of neuropathic and nociceptive pain.

Exercise Solutions for Chronic Pain

Low-Impact Aerobic Exercises

Low-impact aerobic exercises improve cardiovascular health and reduce pain without placing excessive stress on the joints:

- **Walking**: A simple and accessible form of exercise that promotes overall fitness.
- **Cycling**: A low-impact activity that strengthens the lower body and improves cardiovascular endurance.
- **Swimming**: Provides full-body exercise with minimal joint stress due to water buoyancy.

Strengthening and Flexibility Exercises

Building muscle strength and improving flexibility can alleviate chronic pain and enhance functional abilities:

- **Resistance Training**: Using weights, resistance bands, or bodyweight exercises to build muscle strength.
- **Yoga and Pilates**: Practices that combine stretching, strengthening, and relaxation to improve flexibility and reduce pain.
- **Core Strengthening**: Exercises such as planks and bridges to support the spine and reduce back pain.

Mind-Body Exercises

Mind-body exercises integrate physical movement with mental relaxation techniques:

- **Tai Chi**: A gentle form of martial arts that promotes balance, flexibility, and relaxation.
- **Meditation**: Mindfulness practices that reduce stress and improve pain management.

Example: Managing Chronic Lower Back Pain

Chronic lower back pain is a common issue in adults:

- **Core Strengthening**: Exercises such as planks and bridges to support the spine and reduce pain.
- **Flexibility Exercises**: Stretching the hamstrings, hip flexors, and lower back to improve mobility.
- **Aerobic Exercise**: Low-impact activities such as walking or swimming to enhance overall fitness and reduce pain.

Addressing Lifestyle-Related Issues

Work-Related Pain Management

Managing work-related pain involves addressing ergonomic issues and promoting healthy work habits:

- **Ergonomic Adjustments**: Modifying workstations to support proper posture and reduce strain.
- **Frequent Breaks**: Encouraging regular breaks to stand, stretch, and move around.
- **Stress Management**: Incorporating relaxation techniques and stress-reduction strategies.

Chapter 4 – Pain Across the Lifespan

Promoting an Active Lifestyle

Encouraging an active lifestyle can prevent and alleviate pain:

- **Regular Exercise**: Establishing a consistent exercise routine that includes aerobic, strength, and flexibility training.
- **Active Commuting**: Walking or cycling to work to incorporate physical activity into daily routines.
- **Recreational Activities**: Engaging in hobbies and sports that promote movement and enjoyment.

Nutritional Considerations

A balanced diet can support overall health and pain management:

- **Anti-Inflammatory Diet**: Consuming foods rich in omega-3 fatty acids, antioxidants, and whole grains to reduce inflammation.
- **Hydration**: Maintaining proper hydration to support joint health and overall well-being.
- **Weight Management**: Achieving and maintaining a healthy weight to reduce stress on joints and alleviate pain.

Physiotherapy Techniques for Adult Pain

Manual Therapy

Manual therapy techniques can provide pain relief and improve function:

- **Massage Therapy**: Relieving muscle tension and improving circulation.
- **Joint Mobilization**: Techniques to enhance joint mobility and reduce stiffness.

Electrotherapy

Electrotherapy modalities can complement exercise and manual therapy:

- **Transcutaneous Electrical Nerve Stimulation (TENS)**: Reducing pain perception through low-voltage electrical currents.
- **Ultrasound Therapy**: Promoting tissue healing and reducing inflammation with sound waves.

Example: Managing Osteoarthritis Pain

Osteoarthritis is a common condition causing joint pain in adults:

- **Exercise Programs**: Low-impact aerobic exercises, strengthening exercises, and flexibility training to support joint health.
- **Weight Management**: Achieving a healthy weight to reduce stress on affected joints.
- **Manual Therapy**: Techniques to reduce joint stiffness and improve mobility.

Chapter 4 – Pain Across the Lifespan

Conclusion

Managing pain in adulthood requires a comprehensive and individualized approach that addresses the multifaceted nature of chronic pain and lifestyle-related issues. Through targeted exercise solutions, physiotherapy interventions, and lifestyle modifications, adults can achieve long-term pain relief and improved quality of life. By promoting an active lifestyle, addressing ergonomic challenges, and providing ongoing support, physiotherapists play a crucial role in helping adults navigate the complexities of pain management.

Pain in the Elderly: Strategies for Managing Chronic and Acute Pain in Geriatric Populations

Introduction

Pain management in the elderly requires a unique approach that considers age-related changes, comorbidities, and functional limitations. Chronic and acute pain can significantly impact the quality of life and independence of older adults. This chapter explores strategies for managing pain in geriatric populations, highlighting the role of physiotherapy in alleviating pain, enhancing mobility, and promoting overall well-being.

Understanding Geriatric Pain

Types of Pain in the Elderly

Elderly individuals may experience various types of pain:

- **Chronic Pain**: Persistent pain often related to conditions such as arthritis, neuropathy, or osteoporosis.
- **Acute Pain**: Short-term pain resulting from injuries, surgeries, or acute illnesses.
- **Neuropathic Pain**: Pain caused by nerve damage, common in conditions like diabetes or shingles.

Common Causes of Pain in the Elderly

Several factors contribute to pain in older adults:

- **Arthritis**: Degenerative joint disease-causing pain, stiffness, and reduced mobility.
- **Osteoporosis**: A condition leading to fragile bones and increased risk of fractures.
- **Neuropathy**: Nerve damage causing pain, numbness, and tingling sensations.

Chapter 4 – Pain Across the Lifespan

Physiological and Psychological Aspects of Geriatric Pain

Pain in the elderly is influenced by various factors:

- **Age-Related Changes**: Decreased muscle mass, joint degeneration, and reduced bone density.
- **Comorbidities**: Multiple chronic conditions that can complicate pain management.
- **Psychological Factors**: Depression, anxiety, and cognitive impairment can affect pain perception and coping strategies.

Managing Chronic Pain in the Elderly

Understanding Chronic Pain in the Elderly

Chronic pain in older adults requires careful assessment and individualized management:

- **Multimodal Approach**: Combining pharmacological and non-pharmacological interventions.
- **Patient-Centered Care**: Considering the patient's overall health, preferences, and goals.

5
Pain in Special Populations

Athletes and Pain: Optimizing Performance and Recovery through Targeted Exercise Protocols

Introduction

Athletes face unique challenges related to pain due to the high physical demands and competitive nature of sports. Pain management for athletes must balance the need for recovery with the desire to maintain peak performance. This chapter explores targeted exercise protocols designed to optimize both performance and recovery, considering the specific needs of athletes.

Understanding Athletic Pain

Athletic pain can be acute, resulting from a specific injury, or chronic, due to repetitive strain and overuse. It's essential to differentiate between beneficial pain, which indicates muscle adaptation, and detrimental pain, which signals injury. Understanding this distinction is crucial for effective pain management.

Targeted Exercise Protocols

1. Periodization Training:

- Concept: Periodization involves systematic planning of athletic training cycles to optimize performance and recovery. It alternates periods of high intensity with phases of rest and recovery.
- Application: Implementing periodization helps athletes avoid overtraining and reduce the risk of injuries. It includes macro cycles (annual training plans), mesocycles (monthly training plans), and micro cycles (weekly training plans).

2. Eccentric Training:

- Concept: Eccentric exercises focus on the lengthening phase of muscle contraction, known to induce greater muscle damage but also promote significant strength gains and adaptation.
- Application: Used for injury prevention and rehabilitation, particularly for tendon-related issues like Achilles tendinopathy. Incorporating controlled eccentric exercises can improve muscle-tendon resilience.

Chapter 5 – Pain in Special Populations

3. Proprioceptive Training:

- Concept: Proprioceptive training enhances the body's ability to sense its position in space, crucial for balance and coordination.
- Application: Integrates exercises that challenge balance and stability, such as single-leg stands on unstable surfaces. Essential for sports that require rapid changes in direction and agility.

4. High-Intensity Interval Training (HIIT):

- Concept: HIIT involves short bursts of intense activity followed by periods of rest or low-intensity exercise. It improves cardiovascular fitness and endurance.
- Application: HIIT sessions can be tailored to mimic the demands of specific sports, improving both anaerobic and aerobic capacities. Beneficial for sports requiring bursts of high-intensity effort.

5. Active Recovery:

- Concept: Active recovery involves low-intensity exercises that promote blood flow and aid in the removal of metabolic waste from muscles.
- Application: Activities such as light jogging, cycling, or swimming post-training sessions can accelerate recovery processes, reducing muscle soreness and stiffness.

ACTIVITY FOR STUDENTS:

(Student can practice the activity as case scenarios)

- **ACTIVITY 1**: A 25-year-old professional soccer player implemented periodization training, resulting in enhanced performance metrics and reduced injury rates over a competitive season.
- **ACTIVITY 2**: A 30-year-old marathon runner with chronic Achilles tendinopathy benefited from an eccentric training regimen, experiencing reduced pain and improved running efficiency.

Psychological Aspects of Pain Management

Athletes' psychological response to pain and injury significantly impacts their recovery and performance. Integrating psychological support, such as cognitive-behavioural therapy (CBT) and mindfulness practices, can enhance pain tolerance and coping mechanisms.

Chapter 5 – Pain in Special Populations

Conclusion

Optimizing performance and recovery in athletes requires a multifaceted approach that includes targeted exercise protocols, psychological support, and strategic planning. By addressing both the physical and mental aspects of pain, physiotherapists can help athletes achieve peak performance while minimizing injury risks.

Pain in Disabilities: Adaptive Exercise Techniques for Individuals with Physical and Cognitive Disabilities

Introduction

Individuals with disabilities often experience pain due to various physical and cognitive challenges. Adaptive exercise techniques are essential for managing pain and improving overall quality of life. This chapter explores tailored exercise interventions that accommodate specific needs and enhance functional abilities

Understanding Pain in Disabilities

Pain in individuals with disabilities can stem from musculoskeletal imbalances, joint deformities, spasticity, or secondary conditions related to their primary disability. Addressing these unique pain sources requires a comprehensive and individualized approach.

Adaptive Exercise Techniques

1. **Modified Strength Training:**
- Concept: Strength training adapted to individual capabilities, focusing on improving muscle function and reducing pain.
- Application: Utilizing resistance bands, light weights, or body-weight exercises can enhance muscle strength without overloading joints. Tailored programs consider the individual's physical limitations and capabilities.:
2. **Aquatic Therapy:**
- Concept: Exercising in water reduces the load on joints and muscles, providing a low-impact environment for movement.
- Application: Aquatic therapy can improve cardiovascular fitness, muscle strength, and joint flexibility. It is particularly beneficial for individuals with severe physical disabilities or chronic pain conditions.
3. **Neuromuscular Electrical Stimulation (NMES):**
- Concept: NMES uses electrical impulses to stimulate muscle contractions, aiding in muscle strengthening and pain reduction.

- **Application**: NMES can be integrated into exercise routines for individuals with limited voluntary muscle control, enhancing muscle activation and functional abilities.
4. **Adaptive Yoga and Pilates:**
- Concept: Adaptive yoga and Pilates focus on flexibility, strength, and body awareness, modified to accommodate physical limitations.
- Application: Poses and exercises are adapted using props and modifications to ensure safety and effectiveness. These practices can improve pain management, mobility, and overall well-being.
5. **Functional Electrical Stimulation (FES):**
- Concept: FES involves using electrical currents to activate paralyzed or weak muscles, facilitating functional movements.
- Application: FES can be used for activities such as cycling or walking, promoting muscle re-education and reducing pain in individuals with spinal cord injuries or neurological conditions.

Cognitive Disabilities and Pain Management

Individuals with cognitive disabilities, such as autism or intellectual disabilities, may have unique pain experiences and communication challenges. Tailored exercise programs must consider sensory sensitivities, communication barriers, and the need for structured routines.

ACTIVITY FOR STUDENTS

(Students can practice the activity as case scenarios)

- **ACTIVITY 1**: A 35-year-old individual with cerebral palsy experienced improved muscle strength and reduced spasticity after participating in a 12-week aquatic therapy program.
- **ACTIVITY 2**: A 28-year-old with spinal cord injury reported enhanced functional abilities and pain relief after incorporating FES cycling into their rehabilitation routine.

Psychological and Social Support

Integrating psychological and social support into pain management for individuals with disabilities is crucial. This includes family education, support groups, and behavioural therapies to address the emotional and social aspects of living with a disability.

Conclusion

Adaptive exercise techniques offer significant benefits for managing pain and improving functional abilities in individuals with physical and cognitive disabilities. By tailoring interventions to individual needs and incorporating comprehensive support systems, physiotherapists can enhance the quality of life for these populations.

… Chapter 5 – Pain in Special Populations

Post-Surgical Pain: Rehabilitation Exercises to Expedite Recovery and Manage Post-Operative Pain

Introduction

Post-surgical pain is a common and often debilitating experience for patients. Effective rehabilitation exercises are crucial for managing pain and expediting recovery. This chapter explores evidence-based exercise protocols tailored to various types of surgeries, emphasizing pain management and functional restoration.

Understanding Post-Surgical Pain

Post-surgical pain can be acute or evolve into chronic pain if not properly managed. It results from tissue damage, inflammation, and the body's response to surgery. Comprehensive rehabilitation programs must address these factors to facilitate recovery and prevent complications.

Rehabilitation Exercise Protocols

1. Early Mobilization:

- Concept: Initiating movement and physical activity shortly after surgery to prevent complications and promote healing.
- Application: Early mobilization protocols, such as bed exercises, passive range-of-motion exercises, and assisted walking, can reduce the risk of deep vein thrombosis (DVT), pneumonia, and muscle atrophy.

2. Progressive Strengthening:

- Concept: Gradually increasing the intensity and resistance of exercises to rebuild muscle strength and endurance.
- Application: Strengthening exercises should be tailored to the type of surgery and patient's progress. Resistance bands, light weights, and body-weight exercises are commonly used.

3. Flexibility and Range of Motion (ROM) Exercises:

- Concept: Enhancing joint flexibility and range of motion to prevent stiffness and improve function.
- Application: Gentle stretching and ROM exercises are essential for surgeries involving joints, such as knee or shoulder replacements. These exercises help restore mobility and reduce pain.

Chapter 5 – Pain in Special Populations

4. Aerobic Conditioning:

- Concept: Incorporating aerobic exercises to improve cardiovascular health and overall endurance.
- Application: Activities like walking, cycling, or swimming can be gradually introduced as tolerated. Aerobic conditioning supports overall recovery and helps manage post-operative pain.

5. Functional Training:

- Concept: Focusing on exercises that mimic daily activities to enhance functional independence.
- Application: Functional training exercises, such as sit-to-stand transitions, stair climbing, and balance exercises, are crucial for restoring daily activity capabilities and improving quality of life.

Pain Management Strategies

- **Cryotherapy and Thermotherapy**: Applying cold or heat packs can reduce inflammation and alleviate pain. Cold therapy is beneficial immediately post-surgery, while heat therapy can be used in later stages of recovery.
- **Transcutaneous Electrical Nerve Stimulation (TENS)**: TENS units can provide pain relief by stimulating nerves and blocking pain signals. This non-invasive method is useful for managing post-surgical pain without medication.
- **Manual Therapy**: Techniques such as massage, joint mobilization, and soft tissue manipulation can reduce pain, improve circulation, and enhance recovery. Manual therapy should be integrated with exercise protocols for optimal results.

ACTIVITY FOR STUDENTS:

(Student can practice the activity as case scenarios)

- **ACTIVITY 1**: A 50-year-old patient recovering from knee replacement surgery experienced significant improvements in pain and mobility after a 10-week progressive strengthening and ROM exercise program.
- **ACTIVITY 2**: A 45-year-old patient post-spinal fusion surgery reported reduced pain and increased functional capacity following a 12-week rehabilitation program incorporating early mobilization, aerobic conditioning, and functional training exercises.

Psychological Support and Education

Post-surgical pain management also involves addressing psychological factors such as anxiety, depression, and fear of movement. Providing patients with education about their surgery, expected recovery timelines, and pain management techniques can empower them and reduce anxiety. Cognitive-behavioural therapy (CBT) and mindfulness practices can also be integrated to improve mental resilience and pain coping strategies.

Multidisciplinary Approach

A multidisciplinary approach involving physiotherapists, surgeons, pain specialists, and occupational therapists ensures comprehensive care. Coordination among healthcare providers is essential for creating individualized rehabilitation plans that address all aspects of the patient's recovery.

Innovative Technologies in Post-Surgical Rehabilitation

- **Virtual Reality (VR) Therapy**: VR can be used to create immersive environments that distract patients from pain and encourage movement. VR-based rehabilitation exercises have shown promising results in improving pain management and engagement.
- **Wearable Technology**: Wearable devices that monitor physical activity, heart rate, and other vital signs can provide real-time feedback and help track progress. These devices can motivate patients to stay active and adhere to their rehabilitation programs.
- **Tele-rehabilitation**: Remote rehabilitation sessions via video conferencing allow patients to receive guidance and support from physiotherapists without needing to visit a clinic. Tele-rehabilitation is particularly beneficial for patients with limited mobility or those living in remote areas.

Conclusion

Post-surgical rehabilitation exercises play a critical role in managing pain and expediting recovery. By implementing evidence-based protocols tailored to specific surgeries and individual needs, physiotherapists can enhance patient outcomes and promote functional independence. A holistic approach that includes psychological support, innovative technologies, and a multidisciplinary team ensures comprehensive care and optimal recovery for post-surgical patients.

6
Interdisciplinary Perspectives on Pain

The Psychological Dimension of Pain: Incorporating Cognitive-Behavioural Strategies with Physical Therapy

Introduction

Pain is not solely a physical phenomenon; it involves significant psychological components that influence how pain is perceived, managed, and experienced. Integrating cognitive-behavioural strategies with physical therapy offers a holistic approach to pain management, addressing both the mind and body to improve patient outcomes.

Understanding the Psychological Dimension of Pain

Psychological factors such as stress, anxiety, depression, and cognitive distortions can amplify the perception of pain and hinder recovery. Cognitive-behavioural strategies (CBT) aim to alter these psychological factors, thereby reducing pain and improving coping mechanisms.

Cognitive-Behavioural Strategies in Pain Management

1. **Cognitive Restructuring:**
   - Concept: Cognitive restructuring involves identifying and challenging negative thought patterns related to pain and replacing them with more balanced and realistic thoughts.
   - Application: Patients learn to recognize and reframe catastrophic thinking (e.g., "I will never recover") into more positive and achievable goals. This technique helps in reducing anxiety and improving overall pain perception.
2. **Behavioural Activation:**
   - Concept: Behavioural activation focuses on increasing engagement in meaningful activities to counteract the effects of depression and inactivity.
   - Application: Patients are encouraged to gradually resume activities they find enjoyable or fulfilling. This approach helps in reducing pain-related disability and enhancing quality of life.
3. **Mindfulness and Relaxation Techniques:**
   - Concept: Mindfulness and relaxation techniques, such as deep breathing, progressive muscle relaxation, and mindfulness meditation, help in managing pain by reducing stress and promoting relaxation.
   - Application: Incorporating these techniques into physical therapy sessions can help patients manage pain, improve emotional well-being, and enhance overall recovery.

4. **Pain Education:**
   - Concept: Educating patients about the nature of pain, its psychological aspects, and the role of physical therapy in managing pain helps in reducing fear and anxiety.
   - Application: Providing information about pain mechanisms, the impact of stress, and coping strategies empowers patients to take an active role in their recovery.
5. **Goal Setting and Self-Monitoring:**
   - Concept: Setting realistic goals and monitoring progress are essential for motivation and adherence to treatment plans.
   - Application: Patients work with therapists to set specific, measurable, achievable, relevant, and time-bound (SMART) goals. Regular self-monitoring and feedback help in tracking progress and making necessary adjustments.

ACTIVITY FOR STUDENTS:

(Student can practice the activity as case scenarios)

- **ACTIVITY 1**: A 40-year-old patient with chronic lower back pain integrated cognitive restructuring and mindfulness techniques into their physical therapy program, resulting in reduced pain intensity and improved functional abilities.
- **ACTIVITY 2**: A 35-year-old patient with fibromyalgia benefited from behavioural activation and goal setting, reporting increased activity levels, reduced depression, and enhanced quality of life.

Integrating CBT with Physical Therapy

Combining CBT with physical therapy involves collaborative approaches where psychological strategies are used alongside physical exercises. This integrated approach helps in addressing both the physical and psychological aspects of pain, leading to more comprehensive and effective management.

Challenges and Considerations

- Individual Variability: Patients' psychological responses to pain and therapy may vary, requiring personalized approaches.
- Therapist Training: Physical therapists need training in CBT techniques to effectively incorporate them into treatment plans.
- Coordination of Care: Effective integration of CBT with physical therapy requires collaboration between therapists, psychologists, and other healthcare professionals.

Chapter 6 – Interdisciplinary Perspectives on Pain

Conclusion

Incorporating cognitive-behavioural strategies with physical therapy provides a multidimensional approach to pain management, addressing both physical and psychological components. By utilizing techniques such as cognitive restructuring, behavioural activation, and mindfulness, therapists can enhance patient outcomes and support holistic recovery.

Nutrition and Pain: How Diet Influences Pain and Recovery

Introduction

Nutrition plays a crucial role in pain management and recovery. The relationship between diet, inflammation, and pain perception is complex but significant. Understanding how dietary choices impact pain can help in developing comprehensive treatment plans that include nutritional considerations.

The Role of Nutrition in Pain Management

1. **Anti-Inflammatory Diets:**
- Concept: Diets rich in anti-inflammatory foods can help reduce systemic inflammation and alleviate pain.
- Application: Incorporating foods high in omega-3 fatty acids (e.g., fatty fish, flaxseeds), antioxidants (e.g., berries, leafy greens), and polyphenols (e.g., turmeric, green tea) can help manage chronic pain conditions such as arthritis and fibromyalgia.
2. **The Impact of Macronutrients:**
- Proteins: Adequate protein intake supports muscle repair and recovery. High-quality protein sources such as lean meats, legumes, and dairy can aid in managing pain and enhancing physical recovery.
- Carbohydrates: Complex carbohydrates provide sustained energy and help in maintaining stable blood sugar levels. Low glycaemic index foods (e.g., whole grains, vegetables) are beneficial for managing pain and preventing inflammation.
- Fats: Healthy fats, including monounsaturated and polyunsaturated fats, play a role in reducing inflammation. Sources include avocados, nuts, seeds, and olive oil.
3. **Micronutrients and Pain:**
- Vitamin D: Essential for bone health and modulating the immune system. Low vitamin D levels have been linked to increased pain sensitivity. Supplementation may be beneficial for patients with deficiencies.
- Magnesium: Involved in muscle function and nerve transmission. Magnesium deficiency can contribute to muscle cramps and pain. Dietary sources include nuts, seeds, and green leafy vegetables.
- B Vitamins: Important for nerve health and pain modulation. Deficiencies in B vitamins (e.g., B12, B6) can exacerbate neuropathic pain.

4. **Hydration:**
   - Concept: Adequate hydration is essential for maintaining joint lubrication and reducing muscle cramps.
   - Application: Encouraging patients to drink sufficient water and consume hydrating foods (e.g., fruits, vegetables) can support overall health and aid in pain management.
5. **Food Sensitivities and Allergies:**
   - Concept: Certain foods can trigger inflammation or exacerbate pain in individuals with sensitivities or allergies.
   - Application: Identifying and avoiding trigger foods (e.g., gluten, dairy) through elimination diets or testing can help in managing pain and improving symptoms.

ACTIVITY FOR STUDENTS:

(Student can practice the activity as case scenarios)

- **ACTIVITY 1**: A 50-year-old patient with rheumatoid arthritis experienced reduced pain and improved joint function after adopting an anti-inflammatory diet rich in omega-3 fatty acids and antioxidants.
- **ACTIVITY 2:** A 40-year-old individual with chronic migraines reported fewer and less severe episodes after adjusting their diet to include magnesium-rich foods and maintaining proper hydration.

Integrating Nutrition with Physical Therapy

Nutrition and physical therapy can be integrated into a comprehensive treatment plan. Collaboration between dietitians and physiotherapists ensures that dietary recommendations complement exercise regimens, optimizing pain management and recovery.

Challenges and Considerations

- Individual Variability: Nutritional needs and responses to dietary changes can vary among individuals.
- Patient Education: Educating patients about the role of nutrition in pain management is essential for successful implementation.
- Ongoing Research: Continued research is needed to further elucidate the relationship between diet and pain, leading to more personalized dietary recommendations.

Conclusion

Nutrition plays a vital role in managing pain and facilitating recovery. By incorporating anti-inflammatory foods, addressing macronutrient and micronutrient needs, and considering food sensitivities, physiotherapists and dietitians can enhance pain management strategies and support overall well-being.

Technological Innovations: Utilizing Wearable Tech, VR, and AI in Pain Management and Exercise

Introduction

Technological innovations have revolutionized pain management and rehabilitation, offering new tools for assessing, monitoring, and treating pain. Wearable technology, virtual reality (VR), and artificial intelligence (AI) provide advanced solutions to enhance pain management and exercise interventions.

Wearable Technology in Pain Management

1. **Activity Trackers:**
- Concept: Wearable devices that monitor physical activity, sleep patterns, and other health metrics.
- Application: Activity trackers can provide real-time feedback on physical activity levels and adherence to exercise programs. They help in tracking progress and setting achievable goals.
2. **Smart Sensors:**
- Concept: Sensors embedded in wearable's that monitor physiological parameters such as heart rate, muscle activity, and movement.
- Application: Smart sensors can detect abnormal movement patterns or muscle strain, allowing for timely adjustments to exercise regimens and preventing injuries.
3. **Biofeedback Devices:**
- Concept: Devices that provide real-time feedback on physiological functions, such as muscle tension or skin temperature.
- Application: Biofeedback can help patients learn to control physiological responses related to pain, such as muscle relaxation and stress reduction.

Chapter 6 – Interdisciplinary Perspectives on Pain

Virtual Reality (VR) in Pain Management

1. **Immersive Therapy:**
   - Concept: VR creates immersive environments that distract patients from pain and facilitate rehabilitation exercises.
   - Application: VR therapy can be used for pain management during physical therapy sessions, providing engaging and interactive experiences that reduce pain perception and improve motivation.
2. **Exposure Therapy:**
   - Concept: VR exposure therapy involves exposing patients to simulated scenarios that help them confront and manage pain-related fears or anxieties.
   - Application: For patients with chronic pain or post-traumatic stress, VR can provide controlled environments to gradually expose them to feared situations, promoting desensitization and coping.
3. **Rehabilitation Exercises:**
   - Concept: VR-based rehabilitation exercises combine physical activity with virtual challenges to enhance engagement and adherence.
   - Application: VR games and exercises can be tailored to specific rehabilitation goals, such as improving range of motion, strength, and coordination.

Artificial Intelligence (AI) in Pain Management

1. **Predictive Analytics:**
   - Concept: AI algorithms analyze patient data to predict pain levels, treatment outcomes, and potential complications.
   - Application: Predictive analytics can assist in personalizing treatment plans by identifying patterns and trends in pain and recovery, leading to more targeted interventions.
2. **Chatbots and Virtual Assistants:**
   - Concept: AI-powered chatbots and virtual assistants provide real-time support and guidance for pain management and exercise adherence.
   - Application: These tools can answer patient queries, offer educational resources, and provide reminders for medication and exercise, improving engagement and adherence.
3. **AI-Enhanced Imaging:**
   - Concept: AI algorithms analyze medical imaging data to identify and diagnose pain-related conditions more accurately.
   - Application: AI-enhanced imaging can assist in detecting subtle changes in tissues and structures, leading to more precise diagnoses and treatment plans.

Chapter 6 – Interdisciplinary Perspectives on Pain

ACTIVITY FOR STUDENTS:

(Student can practice the activity as case scenarios)

- **ACTIVITY 1**: A 45-year-old patient with chronic low back pain used a wearable activity tracker to monitor their physical activity and adjust their exercise routine, resulting in improved pain management and increased activity levels.
- **ACTIVITY 2**: A 30-year-old individual with post-stroke rehabilitation participated in VR-based therapy, achieving significant improvements in motor function and pain reduction through engaging virtual exercises.

Challenges and Considerations

- **Cost and Accessibility**: Technological innovations may be expensive and not always accessible to all patients.
- **Data Privacy**: Ensuring the privacy and security of patient data collected by wearable devices and AI systems is crucial.
- **Integration with Traditional Therapies**: Technology should complement, not replace, traditional pain management and physical therapy approaches.

Technological innovations such as wearable tech, VR, and AI offer promising advancements in pain management and rehabilitation. By integrating these tools into comprehensive treatment plans, physiotherapists can enhance pain management, improve exercise adherence, and support better patient outcomes. The future of pain management will increasingly rely on these technologies to provide personalized and effective care.

7
Creative And Holistic Approaches

Art and Music Therapy: Integrating Creative Therapies with Exercise for Holistic Pain Management

Introduction

Art and music therapy are increasingly recognized as valuable components of a holistic approach to pain management. These creative therapies can complement traditional physical therapies, offering additional avenues for pain relief and emotional support. This chapter explores how integrating art and music therapy with exercise can enhance pain management and overall well-being.

Art Therapy and Pain Management

1. **Understanding Art Therapy:**
- Concept: Art therapy involves using artistic processes to help individuals express emotions, explore feelings, and gain insight into their pain experiences.
- Application: Techniques include drawing, painting, sculpting, and collage-making. Art therapy can be particularly useful for patients who have difficulty verbalizing their pain or emotions.
2. **Benefits of Art Therapy:**
- Emotional Expression: Art therapy provides a non-verbal outlet for expressing pain and emotions, which can reduce stress and anxiety.
- Distraction and Engagement: Engaging in creative activities can serve as a distraction from pain and improve focus and engagement.
- Self-Reflection and Insight: Creating art allows patients to reflect on their pain experiences and gain new perspectives, fostering personal insight and coping strategies.
3. **Integrating Art Therapy with Exercise:**
- Concept: Combining art therapy with exercise involves incorporating creative activities into rehabilitation programs, enhancing both physical and emotional aspects of recovery.
- Application: For example, patients may use art-based activities as part of their warm-up or cool-down routines. Art therapy can also be used to explore and visualize exercise goals, progress, and achievements.

Chapter 7 – Creative And Holistic Approaches

ACTIVITY FOR STUDENTS:

(Student can practice the activity as case scenarios)

- **ACTIVITY 1**: A 55-year-old patient with chronic pain participated in a combined art and exercise therapy program. Art therapy helped in expressing and processing emotions related to pain, while exercise improved physical function and pain levels.
- **ACTIVITY 2**: A 40-year-old patient with fibromyalgia found that integrating art therapy with gentle stretching exercises improved emotional well-being and reduced pain symptoms.

Music Therapy and Pain Management

1. **Understanding Music Therapy:**
- Concept: Music therapy uses music-based interventions to address physical, emotional, cognitive, and social needs. Techniques include listening to music, playing instruments, and songwriting.
- Application: Music therapy can be adapted to individual preferences and needs, providing a flexible approach to pain management.
2. **Benefits of Music Therapy:**
- Pain Reduction: Research shows that music therapy can reduce pain perception and improve pain management by activating the brain's reward and pleasure centers.
- Relaxation and Stress Reduction: Music has a calming effect that can help reduce stress and anxiety, which can contribute to pain relief.
- Emotional Support: Music therapy can provide emotional support and improve mood, which is beneficial for patients experiencing chronic pain.
3. **Integrating Music Therapy with Exercise:**
- Concept: Combining music therapy with exercise involves using music to enhance the therapeutic experience, improve motivation, and create a more enjoyable exercise environment.
- Application: Patients can listen to preferred music during exercise sessions, or participate in rhythmic exercises and movement activities that incorporate musical elements.

ACTIVITY FOR STUDENTS:

(Student can practice the activity as case scenarios)

- **ACTIVITY 1**: A 60-year-old patient with arthritis used music therapy to complement their exercise program. Music therapy helped reduce pain perception and increase motivation during physical activity.

Chapter 7 – Creative And Holistic Approaches

- **ACTIVITY 2**: A 30-year-old patient recovering from surgery incorporated music therapy into their rehabilitation routine. The combination of music and exercise facilitated a more positive recovery experience and improved overall pain management.

Combining Art and Music Therapy with Physical Therapy

1. **Holistic Approach:**
- Concept: Integrating creative therapies with physical therapy offers a holistic approach to pain management, addressing both physical and emotional aspects of recovery.
- Application: Collaborative care involving art therapists, music therapists, and physiotherapists can create personalized treatment plans that incorporate creative therapies into exercise routines.
2. **Personalization and Flexibility:**
- Concept: Tailoring creative therapies to individual preferences and needs enhances engagement and effectiveness.
- Application: Assessing patients' interests and preferences in art and music can help in designing personalized interventions that align with their therapeutic goals.
3. Challenges and Considerations:
- Individual Preferences: Not all patients may be receptive to art or music therapy, requiring flexibility and alternative approaches.
- Training and Expertise: Therapists may need specialized training to effectively integrate creative therapies with physical therapy.

Conclusion

Art and music therapy offer valuable tools for holistic pain management when combined with physical therapy. By addressing emotional expression, distraction, and motivation, these creative therapies enhance the overall therapeutic experience and support comprehensive recovery. Integrating art and music therapy with exercise provides a well-rounded approach to managing pain and improving quality of life.

Mind-Body Connection: Techniques like Yoga, Pilates, and Mindfulness in Pain Relief

Introduction

The mind-body connection plays a crucial role in pain management, with techniques such as yoga, Pilates, and mindfulness offering effective strategies for reducing pain and enhancing overall well-being. This chapter explores how these mind-body techniques can be integrated into pain management programs to address both physical and psychological aspects of pain.

Chapter 7 – Creative And Holistic Approaches

Yoga and Pain Management

1. **Understanding Yoga:**
   - Concept: Yoga combines physical postures, breath control, and meditation to promote physical health, mental clarity, and emotional balance.
   - Application: Yoga techniques can be adapted to accommodate different pain conditions and physical limitations, making it a versatile tool for pain management.
2. **Benefits of Yoga:**
   - Pain Reduction: Yoga can reduce pain by improving flexibility, strength, and balance, and by promoting relaxation and stress reduction.
   - Improved Functionality: Regular practice of yoga can enhance functional abilities and reduce disability associated with chronic pain conditions.
   - Mind-Body Integration: Yoga emphasizes the connection between mind and body, helping patients develop greater awareness and control over their pain experiences.
3. **Yoga Poses and Techniques:**
   - Gentle Poses: For individuals with chronic pain, gentle poses such as child's pose, cat-cow, and seated forward bend can provide relief and improve mobility.
   - Breath-work: Techniques such as diaphragmatic breathing and alternate nostril breathing can help manage stress and promote relaxation.
   - Meditation: Mindfulness meditation and guided imagery can help patients manage pain by reducing stress and enhancing emotional resilience.

ACTIVITY FOR STUDENTS:

(Student can practice the activity as case scenarios)

- **ACTIVITY 1**: A 50-year-old patient with lower back pain incorporated a tailored yoga program into their rehabilitation, experiencing reduced pain and improved mobility.
- **ACTIVITY 2**: A 40-year-old patient with arthritis used yoga and breathwork techniques to manage pain and enhance overall quality of life.

Pilates and Pain Management

1. **Understanding Pilates:**
   - Concept: Pilates focuses on core strength, flexibility, and postural alignment through controlled movements and exercises.
   - Application: Pilates exercises can be adapted to address specific pain conditions and improve overall functional capacity.
2. **Benefits of Pilates:**
   - Core Strength: Strengthening the core muscles can provide better support for the spine and reduce pain associated with poor posture and muscle imbalances.

Chapter 7 – Creative And Holistic Approaches

- Flexibility and Alignment: Pilates improves flexibility and alignment, which can alleviate pain related to joint stiffness and muscle tightness.
- Posture and Balance: Enhancing posture and balance through Pilates exercises can reduce the risk of falls and injuries, contributing to better pain management.

3. **Pilates Exercises and Techniques:**

- Reformer Exercises: Using a Pilates reformer machine can provide resistance and support for a range of exercises that target core strength and flexibility.
- Mat Exercises: Floor-based exercises such as leg circles, plank variations, and bridging can be effective for improving strength and stability.
- Breathing Techniques: Integrating breathing techniques into Pilates practice can enhance relaxation and support proper movement patterns.

ACTIVITY FOR STUDENTS:

(Student can practice the activity as case scenarios)

- **ACTIVITY 1**: A 45-year-old patient with chronic neck pain benefited from a Pilates program focused on improving core strength and posture, leading to reduced pain and improved function.
- **ACTIVITY 2**: A 35-year-old patient with hip pain experienced relief and improved mobility after incorporating Pilates exercises into their rehabilitation routine.

Mindfulness and Pain Management

1. **Understanding Mindfulness:**
- Concept: Mindfulness involves paying attention to the present moment with acceptance and non-judgment. Techniques include mindfulness meditation, body scan, and mindful movement.
- Application: Mindfulness practices can help patients manage pain by enhancing self-awareness, reducing stress, and promoting relaxation.

2. **Benefits of Mindfulness:**
- Pain Perception: Mindfulness can alter the way pain is perceived, reducing the emotional and cognitive impact of pain.
- Stress Reduction: By reducing stress and anxiety, mindfulness can help in managing pain more effectively.
- Emotional Regulation: Mindfulness practices enhance emotional resilience, helping patients cope with pain-related challenges.

3. **Mindfulness Techniques:**
- Mindfulness Meditation: Practicing mindfulness meditation involves focusing on the breath, bodily sensations, or a specific object to cultivate awareness and relaxation.

Chapter 7 – Creative And Holistic Approaches

- Body Scan: A body scan involves systematically focusing on different areas of the body to increase awareness and identify areas of tension or pain.
- Mindful Movement: Incorporating mindfulness into movement practices, such as walking or gentle stretching, can enhance body awareness and reduce pain.

ACTIVITY FOR STUDENTS:

(Student can practice the activity as case scenarios)

- **ACTIVITY 1**: A 60-year-old patient with chronic pain used mindfulness meditation to manage pain and improve emotional well-being, leading to enhanced quality of life.
- **ACTIVITY 2**: A 30-year-old patient with anxiety-related pain found relief through body scan techniques and mindful movement, improving overall pain management and relaxation.

Integrating Mind-Body Techniques with Physical Therapy

1. **Holistic Approach:**
- Concept: Combining yoga, Pilates, and mindfulness with physical therapy offers a comprehensive approach to pain management, addressing both physical and psychological aspects.
- Application: Personalized treatment plans that incorporate mind-body techniques can enhance therapeutic outcomes and support holistic recovery.
2. **Personalization and Flexibility:**
- Concept: Tailoring mind-body techniques to individual needs and preferences enhances effectiveness and engagement.
- Application: Assessing patients' interests and abilities in yoga, Pilates, and mindfulness helps in designing personalized interventions that align with their therapeutic goals.
3. **Challenges and Considerations:**
- Individual Variability: Responses to mind-body techniques can vary among individuals, requiring flexibility and adaptation.
- Training and Expertise: Therapists may need specialized training to effectively integrate mind-body techniques with physical therapy.

Conclusion

Mind-body techniques such as yoga, Pilates, and mindfulness offer valuable tools for pain management and holistic recovery. By integrating these techniques into physical therapy programs, therapists can address both physical and psychological aspects of pain, enhancing overall well-being and quality of life.

Chapter 7 – Creative And Holistic Approaches

Environmental Influences: How Changing the Physical and Social Environment Can Impact Pain Perception and Recovery

Introduction

The physical and social environment plays a significant role in pain perception and recovery. By understanding and modifying environmental factors, therapists can create supportive and healing environments that enhance pain management and promote recovery.

Physical Environment and Pain Management

1. **Therapeutic Spaces:**
   - Concept: The design and atmosphere of therapeutic spaces, such as clinics and rehabilitation centres, can impact patient comfort and recovery.
   - Application: Creating calming and aesthetically pleasing environments with natural light, comfortable furnishings, and soothing colours can reduce stress and enhance therapeutic outcomes.

2. **Home Environment:**
   - Concept: The home environment significantly affects daily functioning and pain management. Accessibility, safety, and comfort are key factors.
   - Application: Modifying the home environment to include supportive equipment (e.g., grab bars, ergonomic furniture) and creating a safe and organized space can improve functional abilities and reduce pain.

3. **Environmental Modifications for Pain Relief:**
   - Concept: Making environmental adjustments, such as reducing noise levels, controlling temperature, and ensuring proper lighting, can contribute to pain relief and comfort.
   - Application: Implementing these modifications in therapeutic and home settings can enhance relaxation and reduce pain perception.

ACTIVITY FOR STUDENTS:

(Student can practice the activity as case scenarios)

- **ACTIVITY 1**: A patient with chronic pain experienced improved comfort and reduced pain levels after modifications were made to their home environment, including ergonomic furniture and improved lighting.
- **ACTIVITY 2**: A rehabilitation clinic redesigned its physical space to create a more calming environment, resulting in increased patient satisfaction and improved therapeutic outcomes.

Chapter 7 – Creative And Holistic Approaches

Social Environment and Pain Management

1. **Support Systems:**
   - Concept: Social support from family, friends, and caregivers plays a crucial role in pain management and recovery.
   - Application: Encouraging and fostering strong support systems can enhance emotional well-being, provide practical assistance, and improve adherence to treatment plans.
2. **Social Interactions:**
   - Concept: Positive social interactions and engagement can contribute to better pain management and emotional support.
   - Application: Promoting social activities, support groups, and community involvement can enhance patients' overall well-being and coping strategies.
3. **Work and Social Environment:**
   - Concept: The work and social environment can impact pain perception and recovery, particularly for individuals with chronic pain conditions.
   - Application: Implementing workplace accommodations, such as ergonomic adjustments and flexible work arrangements, can support individuals in managing pain and maintaining productivity.

ACTIVITY FOR STUDENTS:

(Student can practice the activity as case scenarios)

- **ACTIVITY 1**: A patient with chronic pain benefited from a support group and social interactions, leading to improved emotional well-being and enhanced coping strategies.
- **ACTIVITY 2**: An individual with a physically demanding job experienced reduced pain and improved recovery after workplace accommodations were made to address ergonomic concerns.

Integrating Environmental Modifications with Physical Therapy

1. **Holistic Approach:**
   - Concept: Combining environmental modifications with physical therapy offers a comprehensive approach to pain management, addressing both physical and social aspects.
   - Application: Personalized treatment plans that include environmental considerations can enhance therapeutic outcomes and support holistic recovery.
2. **Personalization and Flexibility:**
   - Concept: Tailoring environmental modifications to individual needs and preferences enhances effectiveness and comfort.
   - Application: Assessing patients' home and social environments helps in designing personalized interventions that align with their therapeutic goals.

3. **Challenges and Considerations:**
   - Individual Variability: Responses to environmental modifications can vary among individuals, requiring flexibility and adaptation.
   - Collaboration: Effective integration of environmental modifications with physical therapy requires collaboration between therapists, patients, and caregivers.

Conclusion

Environmental influences play a significant role in pain perception and recovery. By understanding and modifying both physical and social environments, therapists can create supportive and healing spaces that enhance pain management and promote overall well-being. Integrating environmental considerations with physical therapy offers a comprehensive approach to managing pain and supporting holistic recovery.

8
Case Studies and Clinical Applications

Real-Life Narratives: Detailed Case Studies Demonstrating Successful Pain Management through Exercise

Introduction

Case studies offer valuable insights into real-life applications of exercise in pain management. By examining detailed narratives of individuals who have successfully managed pain through exercise, this chapter aims to highlight effective strategies, therapeutic approaches, and outcomes that can inform and inspire practice.

Case Study 1: Chronic Lower Back Pain

1. Patient Background:
   - Name: John
   - Age: 52
   - Occupation: Desk job
   - Diagnosis: Chronic lower back pain
2. Initial Presentation:
   - Symptoms: Persistent lower back pain, stiffness, and limited mobility.
   - Impact: Difficulty performing daily activities and reduced quality of life.
3. Treatment Approach:
   - Exercise Program: A combination of stretching, strengthening, and low-impact aerobic exercises.
   - Stretching: Focused on hamstring, hip flexor, and lower back stretches.
   - Strengthening: Core strengthening exercises, including planks and bridges.
   - Aerobic Exercise: Low-impact activities like swimming and walking.
   - Frequency: 3 sessions per week, with progressive increases in intensity.
4. Outcomes:
   - Pain Reduction: Significant reduction in pain levels and improvement in mobility.
   - Functionality: Enhanced ability to perform daily activities and return to a more active lifestyle.
   - Long-Term Maintenance: Continued exercise program with emphasis on self-management and preventive measures.

Chapter 8 – Case Studies and Clinical Applications

5. Lessons Learned:
   - Importance of a Multidimensional Approach: Combining different types of exercises addressed various aspects of pain and functional limitations.
   - Patient Engagement: Active involvement and adherence to the exercise program were crucial for success.

Case Study 2: Post-Surgical Rehabilitation

1. Patient Background:
   - Name: Emily
   - Age: 38
   - Occupation: Teacher
   - Diagnosis: Post-surgical rehabilitation following knee arthroscopy
2. Initial Presentation:
   - Symptoms: Pain, swelling, and reduced range of motion following surgery.
   - Impact: Difficulty with walking and performing daily tasks.
3. Treatment Approach:
   - Exercise Program: Focused on range-of-motion exercises, strengthening, and functional activities.
   - Range-of-Motion Exercises: Gentle knee flexion and extension exercises.
   - Strengthening: Quadriceps and hamstring strengthening exercises using resistance bands.
   - Functional Activities: Gradual progression to weight-bearing activities and balance exercises.
   - Frequency: Daily sessions initially, with gradual reduction as progress was made.
4. Outcomes:
   - Pain Management: Effective pain control through tailored exercises and gradual progression.
   - Recovery: Significant improvements in knee function, strength, and ability to return to normal activities.
   - Patient Satisfaction: High levels of satisfaction with the rehabilitation process and outcomes.
5. Lessons Learned:
   - Gradual Progression: Importance of a gradual approach to avoid overloading the healing tissues and ensure optimal recovery.
   - Individualization: Tailoring the exercise program to the specific needs and goals of the patient.

Chapter 8 – Case Studies and Clinical Applications

Case Study 3: Fibromyalgia Management

1. Patient Background:
   - Name: Linda
   - Age: 45
   - Occupation: Graphic designer
   - Diagnosis: Fibromyalgia
2. Initial Presentation:
   - Symptoms: Widespread musculoskeletal pain, fatigue, and sleep disturbances.
   - Impact: Significant impact on daily functioning and quality of life.
3. Treatment Approach:
   - Exercise Program: Low-impact aerobic exercise, flexibility training, and strength training.
   - Aerobic Exercise: Activities such as cycling and water aerobics.
   - Flexibility Training: Gentle stretching exercises, including yoga and Pilates.
   - Strength Training: Light resistance exercises focusing on major muscle groups.
   - Frequency: 5 sessions per week, with emphasis on consistency and gradual progression.
4. Outcomes:
   - Pain Reduction: Reduction in pain levels and improved overall well-being.
   - Functionality: Enhanced ability to perform daily tasks and improved energy levels.
   - Quality of Life: Improvement in quality of life and reduced impact of symptoms on daily living.
5. Lessons Learned:
   - Consistency: Importance of maintaining a regular exercise routine for managing chronic conditions.
   - Holistic Approach: Combining different types of exercises addressed various symptoms and contributed to overall improvement.

Case Study 4: Osteoarthritis Management

1. Patient Background:
   - Name: Robert
   - Age: 62
   - Occupation: Retired
   - Diagnosis: Osteoarthritis of the hip
2. Initial Presentation:
   - Symptoms: Hip pain, stiffness, and limited mobility.
   - Impact: Difficulty with walking and performing household activities.

3. Treatment Approach:
   - Exercise Program: Focused on low-impact aerobic exercise, strengthening, and flexibility.
   - Aerobic Exercise: Swimming and cycling to improve cardiovascular health without stressing the joints.
   - Strengthening: Hip and thigh muscle strengthening exercises using resistance bands.
   - Flexibility: Gentle stretching exercises to improve joint mobility.
   - Frequency: 4 sessions per week, with gradual increases in intensity.
4. Outcomes:
   - Pain Management: Effective reduction in pain levels and improvement in joint function.
   - Functionality: Enhanced mobility and ability to engage in daily activities with greater ease.
   - Patient Satisfaction: Positive feedback regarding improvements in overall health and quality of life.
5. Lessons Learned:
   - Joint Protection: Importance of using low-impact exercises to protect the joints while improving overall fitness.
   - Consistency and Progression: Need for consistent exercise and gradual progression to achieve long-term benefits.

Conclusion

The real-life narratives presented in these case studies illustrate the diverse applications of exercise in managing various pain conditions. By highlighting different approaches and outcomes, these case studies offer practical insights and inspire effective strategies for pain management through exercise.

Clinical Protocols: Practical Guides and Step-by-Step Protocols for Various Pain Conditions

Introduction

Clinical protocols provide structured and evidence-based guidelines for managing pain through exercise. This section outlines practical protocols for different pain conditions, offering step-by-step approaches to ensure effective and consistent care.

Chapter 8 – Case Studies and Clinical Applications

Protocol 1: Chronic Lower Back Pain

1. Assessment:
   - Initial Evaluation: Assess pain level, range of motion, strength, and functional limitations.
   - Goal Setting: Establish short-term and long-term goals for pain reduction and functional improvement.
2. Exercise Program:
   - Warm-Up (5-10 minutes): Light aerobic activity such as walking or cycling.
   - Stretching (10 minutes): Focus on hamstrings, hip flexors, and lower back.
   - Strengthening (15-20 minutes): Core exercises including planks, bridges, and bird-dogs.
   - Low-Impact Aerobic Exercise (20-30 minutes): Swimming or walking, 3-4 times per week.
   - Cool-Down (5-10 minutes): Gentle stretching and relaxation techniques.
3. Progression:
   - Frequency: Start with 2-3 sessions per week, increasing to 4-5 sessions as tolerated.
   - Intensity: Gradually increase the intensity of exercises based on patient progress and feedback.
4. Monitoring and Evaluation:
   - Regular Check-Ins: Assess progress every 4-6 weeks and adjust the program as needed.
   - Outcome Measures: Use tools such as the Visual Analog Scale (VAS) for pain and functional questionnaires.
5. Patient Education:
   - Self-Management: Educate patients on self-care techniques, including posture and body mechanics.
   - Activity Modification: Provide guidance on modifying daily activities to reduce pain and prevent exacerbations.

Protocol 2: Post-Surgical Rehabilitation

1. Assessment:
   - Initial Evaluation: Assess surgical site, pain levels, range of motion, and functional limitations.
   - Goal Setting: Establish goals for pain management, range of motion, and functional recovery.
2. Exercise Program:
   Phase 1: Early Rehabilitation (Weeks 1-4):
   - Range-of-Motion Exercises (5-10 minutes): Gentle movements to restore flexibility.
   - Isometric Exercises (10-15 minutes): Static contractions to maintain muscle strength without joint movement.

Chapter 8 – Case Studies and Clinical Applications

Phase 2: Intermediate Rehabilitation (Weeks 5-8):

- Strengthening Exercises (15-20 minutes): Focus on improving muscle strength around the surgical site.
- Functional Activities (15-20 minutes): Gradual progression to weight-bearing and functional movements.

Phase 3: Advanced Rehabilitation (Weeks 9-12):

- Advanced strengthening (20-30 minutes): Include resistance training and higher intensity exercises.
- Sport-Specific or Task-Specific Training (20-30 minutes): Prepare for return to specific activities.

3. Progression:
   - Frequency: Begin with daily sessions and adjust based on patient progress and tolerance.
   - Intensity: Gradually increase the intensity and complexity of exercises as healing progresses.
4. Monitoring and Evaluation:
   - Regular Check-Ins: Monitor progress and adjust the program every 2-4 weeks.
   - Outcome Measures: Use tools such as range of motion measurements, strength assessments, and functional tests.
5. Patient Education:
   - Post- Surgical Care: Educate patients on wound care, activity restrictions, and signs of complications.
   - Home Exercise Program: Provide a structured home exercise program to support continued recovery.

Protocol 3: Fibromyalgia Management

1. Assessment:
   - Initial Evaluation: Assess pain levels, fatigue, sleep patterns, and functional limitations.
   - Goal Setting: Establish goals for pain reduction, improved energy levels, and enhanced functionality.
2. Exercise Program:
   - Warm-Up (5-10 minutes): Gentle aerobic activity such as walking or cycling.
   - Aerobic Exercise (20-30 minutes): Low-impact activities like swimming, cycling, or brisk walking, 5 times per week.
   - Flexibility Training (15-20 minutes): Gentle stretching and yoga to improve flexibility and reduce muscle tension.
   - Strength Training (15-20 minutes): Light resistance exercises focusing on major muscle groups, 2-3 times per week.
   - Cool-Down (5-10 minutes): Gentle stretching and relaxation techniques.

Chapter 8 – Case Studies and Clinical Applications

3. Progression:
   - Frequency: Maintain regular exercise routine with gradual increases in intensity and duration.
   - Intensity: Start with lower intensity and increase based on patient feedback and tolerance.
4. Monitoring and Evaluation:
   - Regular Check-Ins: Assess progress every 4-6 weeks and adjust the program as needed.
   - Outcome Measures: Use tools such as the Fibromyalgia Impact Questionnaire (FIQ) and self-reported pain scales.
5. Patient Education:
   - Self-Care: Educate patients on managing fatigue, stress, and sleep disturbances.
   - Lifestyle Modifications: Provide guidance on pacing activities and incorporating relaxation techniques.

Protocol 4: Osteoarthritis Management

1. Assessment:
   - Initial Evaluation: Assess pain levels, joint function, and mobility.
   - Goal Setting: Establish goals for pain management, joint function, and activity levels.
2. Exercise Program:
   - Warm-Up (5-10 minutes): Low-impact aerobic activity such as walking or cycling.
   - Aerobic Exercise (20-30 minutes): Activities like swimming, cycling, or walking, 3-4 times per week.
   - Strength Training (15-20 minutes): Focus on strengthening muscles around affected joints using resistance bands or light weights.
   - Flexibility Training (10-15 minutes): Gentle stretching exercises to maintain or improve joint range of motion.
   - Cool-Down (5-10 minutes): Gentle stretching and relaxation techniques.
3. Progression:
   - Frequency: Maintain regular exercise routine with gradual increases in intensity and duration.
   - Intensity: Adjust exercises based on patient feedback and functional improvements.
4. Monitoring and Evaluation:
   - Regular Check-Ins: Assess progress every 4-6 weeks and adjust the program as needed.
   - Outcome Measures: Use tools such as the Western Ontario and McMaster Universities Osteoarthritis Index (WOMAC) and pain scales.
5. Patient Education:
   - Joint Protection: Educate patients on joint protection strategies and proper body mechanics.
   - Activity Modification: Provide guidance on modifying activities to reduce joint stress and prevent exacerbations.

Conclusion

The clinical protocols outlined in this chapter provide practical, evidence-based guidelines for managing various pain conditions through exercise. By following these step-by-step approaches, therapists can deliver effective and consistent care, improving outcomes and enhancing patients' quality of life.

9

Future Directions in Pain Management

Emerging Trends: Cutting-Edge Research and Future Possibilities in Pain Management and Physiotherapy

Introduction

The field of pain management and physiotherapy is rapidly evolving, with new research and technological advancements continually shaping how pain is understood and treated. This chapter explores the latest trends and future possibilities in pain management, highlighting emerging research, innovative technologies, and potential shifts in clinical practice.

Advances in Pain Pathophysiology

1. **Genomic Research:**
   - Concept: Understanding genetic factors that influence pain sensitivity and response to treatment.
   - Research Focus: Identifying genetic markers associated with chronic pain conditions and personalized medicine approaches.
   - Future Possibilities: Development of tailored therapies based on genetic profiles to improve efficacy and reduce side effects.
2. **Neuroplasticity and Pain:**
   - Concept: Exploring how changes in the nervous system contribute to chronic pain and recovery.
   - Research Focus: Investigating neuroplastic changes in response to pain and rehabilitation.
   - Future Possibilities: Targeted interventions that promote positive neuroplasticity and support recovery from chronic pain.
3. **Pain Modulation Mechanisms:**
   - Concept: Understanding endogenous pain modulation systems and their role in pain perception.
   - Research Focus: Investigating mechanisms such as the descending pain control system and endogenous opioids.
   - Future Possibilities: Development of novel analgesics and interventions that enhance natural pain modulation.

Chapter 9 – Future Directions in Pain Management

Technological Innovations

1. **Wearable Technology:**
   - Concept: Using wearable devices to monitor pain and provide real-time feedback.
   - Current Trends: Development of wearable sensors that track physiological markers of pain and activity levels.
   - Future Possibilities: Integration of AI algorithms to analyze data and provide personalized pain management recommendations.
2. **Virtual Reality (VR):**
   - Concept: Utilizing immersive VR environments for pain management and rehabilitation.
   - Current Trends: Applications in pain distraction during medical procedures and rehabilitation for motor recovery.
   - Future Possibilities: Enhanced VR platforms for personalized pain management and integration with other therapeutic modalities.
3. **Artificial Intelligence (AI) and Machine Learning:**
   - Concept: Leveraging AI and machine learning to predict, diagnose, and treat pain conditions.
   - Current Trends: Development of AI algorithms for pain assessment and personalized treatment planning.
   - Future Possibilities: Advanced AI systems that provide real-time, adaptive treatment recommendations based on patient data.

Integrative and Personalized Medicine

1. **Precision Medicine:**
   - Concept: Tailoring pain management strategies to individual patients based on genetic, environmental, and lifestyle factors.
   - Current Trends: Implementation of personalized treatment plans based on comprehensive patient profiles.
   - Future Possibilities: Expanded use of precision medicine to address complex and multifaceted pain conditions.
2. **Integrative Approaches:**
   - Concept: Combining conventional pain management techniques with complementary therapies.
   - Current Trends: Use of modalities such as acupuncture, massage, and mindfulness in pain management.
   - Future Possibilities: Development of integrative care models that combine multiple therapeutic approaches for enhanced outcomes.

Chapter 9 – Future Directions in Pain Management

3. **Patient-Centred Care:**
   - Concept: Emphasizing patient preferences, values, and involvement in decision-making.
   - Current Trends: Adoption of patient-centred approaches in pain management and rehabilitation.
   - Future Possibilities: Increased focus on patient empowerment, shared decision-making, and holistic care models.

Innovations in Rehabilitation

1. **Robotic-Assisted Therapy:**
   - Concept: Using robotic devices to support rehabilitation and enhance recovery.
   - Current Trends: Development of robotic exoskeletons and rehabilitation robots for motor recovery.
   - Future Possibilities: Advanced robotic systems with improved functionality and accessibility for diverse patient populations.
2. **Biofeedback and Neuro-feedback:**
   - Concept: Utilizing biofeedback and neurofeedback to enhance pain management and rehabilitation.
   - Current Trends: Applications in monitoring physiological responses and training self-regulation techniques.
   - Future Possibilities: Integration of biofeedback and neurofeedback with other therapeutic modalities for comprehensive care.
3. **Telemedicine and Remote Rehabilitation:**
   - Concept: Using telemedicine platforms for remote assessment and rehabilitation.
   - Current Trends: Expansion of telehealth services for pain management and physical therapy.
   - Future Possibilities: Advanced telemedicine platforms with interactive features and real-time monitoring capabilities.

Ethical and Practical Considerations

1. **Data Privacy and Security:**
   - Concept: Ensuring the protection of patient data in the era of digital health technologies.
   - Current Trends: Implementation of data protection measures and compliance with regulations.
   - Future Possibilities: Continued development of secure data management practices and technologies.

Chapter 9 – Future Directions in Pain Management

2. **Accessibility and Equity:**
   - Concept: Addressing disparities in access to pain management and rehabilitation technologies.
   - Current Trends: Efforts to improve access to innovative treatments and technologies for underserved populations.
   - Future Possibilities: Development of strategies and policies to ensure equitable access to emerging pain management solutions.

Conclusion

Emerging trends and future possibilities in pain management and physiotherapy highlight the dynamic nature of the field. Advances in pain pathophysiology, technological innovations, integrative and personalized medicine, and rehabilitation practices offer exciting opportunities for improving pain management and enhancing patient outcomes. By staying informed about these developments, clinicians can adapt and refine their approaches to provide cutting-edge care.

Innovative Practices: How Future Advancements Might Reshape Pain Management and Rehabilitation

Introduction

Future advancements in pain management and rehabilitation have the potential to revolutionize how pain is treated and managed. This chapter explores innovative practices that are likely to reshape the field, focusing on emerging technologies, novel therapeutic approaches, and evolving clinical practices.

Next-Generation Pain Therapies

1. **Gene Therapy:**
   - Concept: Using gene editing techniques to address genetic factors contributing to pain conditions.
   - Current Developments: Research into gene therapy for pain relief and modulation of pain pathways.
   - Future Impact: Potential for targeted interventions that address the root causes of pain at the genetic level.
2. **Regenerative Medicine:**
   - Concept: Utilizing stem cell therapy and tissue engineering for pain management and tissue repair.
   - Current Developments: Clinical trials exploring the use of stem cells for treating chronic pain and promoting healing.
   - Future Impact: Advancement of regenerative therapies to enhance recovery and potentially cure certain pain conditions.

Chapter 9 – Future Directions in Pain Management

3. **Biological Agents:**
   - Concept: Developing biologic agents, such as monoclonal antibodies and cytokine inhibitors, for pain management.
   - Current Developments: Research into biologic treatments for conditions like neuropathic pain and arthritis.
   - Future Impact: Introduction of new biologic therapies that provide targeted and effective pain relief with fewer side effects.

Advanced Diagnostic and Monitoring Tools

1. **Functional Imaging Techniques:**
   - Concept: Utilizing advanced imaging technologies to visualize pain pathways and assess treatment responses.
   - Current Developments: Use of functional MRI and PET scans to study pain mechanisms and monitor therapeutic effects.
   - Future Impact: Enhanced diagnostic capabilities for more precise pain assessment and personalized treatment planning.
2. **Smart Sensors and Wearables:**
   - Concept: Implementing smart sensors and wearable devices to monitor pain levels and physical activity.
   - Current Developments: Development of wearable sensors that provide real-time feedback on physiological markers of pain.
   - Future Impact: Integration of wearable technology with mobile health applications for continuous monitoring and management.
3. **Predictive Analytics:**
   - Concept: Using predictive analytics and AI to forecast pain trajectories and treatment outcomes.
   - Current Developments: Application of machine learning algorithms to analyze patient data and predict pain patterns.
   - Future Impact: Improved ability to anticipate pain flare-ups and adjust treatment plans proactively.

Novel Therapeutic Modalities

1. **Neurostimulation Technologies:**
   - Concept: Exploring advanced neurostimulation techniques for pain relief, such as spinal cord stimulation and transcranial magnetic stimulation.
   - Current Developments: Research into new neurostimulation devices and protocols for chronic pain management.
   - Future Impact: Expanded use of neurostimulation technologies with enhanced precision and customization.

2. **Pharmacogenomics:**
   - Concept: Tailoring pharmacological treatments based on individual genetic profiles to optimize pain management.
   - Current Developments: Studies on genetic variations affecting drug metabolism and response to pain medications.
   - Future Impact: Personalized medication strategies that improve efficacy and reduce adverse effects.
3. **Enhanced Physical Therapy Techniques:**
   - Concept: Innovating physical therapy approaches with advanced equipment and methodologies.
   - Current Developments: Use of robotic-assisted therapy, virtual reality, and biofeedback in rehabilitation.
   - Future Impact: Integration of cutting-edge technologies to enhance therapeutic outcomes and patient engagement.

Evolution of Clinical Practices

1. **Multidisciplinary Care Models:**
   - Concept: Adopting integrated care models that involve collaboration among various healthcare professionals.
   - Current Developments: Implementation of multidisciplinary teams in pain management and rehabilitation.
   - Future Impact: Improved coordination of care and comprehensive treatment plans addressing multiple aspects of pain.
2. **Patient Empowerment and Self-Management:**
   - Concept: Promoting patient involvement in their own pain management through education and self-care strategies.
   - Current Developments: Development of patient education programs and self-management tools.
   - Future Impact: Increased patient empowerment leading to better adherence to treatment plans and improved outcomes.
3. **Health Systems and Policy Changes:**
   - Concept: Evolving healthcare systems and policies to support innovative pain management practices.
   - Current Developments: Policy changes aimed at improving access to new therapies and technologies.
   - Future Impact: Enhanced support for the implementation of innovative practices and equitable access to advanced treatments.

Ethical and Practical Considerations

1. **Ethical Implications of New Technologies:**
   - Concept: Addressing ethical concerns related to emerging technologies in pain management.
   - Current Developments: Discussions on privacy, consent, and equity in the use of advanced technologies.
   - Future Impact: Development of ethical guidelines and policies to ensure responsible use of new innovations.
2. **Cost and Accessibility:**
   - Concept: Ensuring that advancements in pain management are affordable and accessible to all patients.
   - Current Developments: Efforts to address cost barriers and improve access to new treatments.
   - Future Impact: Strategies to reduce disparities and ensure equitable access to innovative therapies.
3. **Training and Education:**
   - Concept: Preparing healthcare professionals for the integration of new technologies and practices.
   - Current Developments: Development of training programs and educational resources for emerging practices.
   - Future Impact: Improved professional competence and readiness to implement cutting-edge pain management techniques.

Conclusion

Innovative practices and future advancements hold the potential to transform pain management and rehabilitation. By embracing new technologies, novel therapies, and evolving clinical practices, the field can achieve significant improvements in pain relief and patient outcomes. Continued research, ethical considerations, and practical implementation will be key to realizing the full potential of these advancements.

10
Conclusion

Integrative Summary: Bringing Together Interdisciplinary Insights and Innovative Practices to Present a Cohesive Approach to Pain Management

Introduction

As we navigate the complexities of pain management, it is crucial to integrate insights from various disciplines and embrace innovative practices to develop a comprehensive and cohesive approach. This chapter synthesizes the interdisciplinary insights and innovative practices discussed throughout the book, presenting a unified strategy for effective pain management. By combining advances in research, technology, and clinical practice, we can enhance patient outcomes and foster a more holistic approach to pain management.

Integrating Multidisciplinary Insights

1. **The Role of Physiotherapy in Pain Management:**
   - Evidence-Based Approaches: Physiotherapy plays a central role in managing pain through evidence-based practices, including exercise therapy, manual techniques, and patient education. Physiotherapists must stay informed about the latest research and techniques to optimize treatment outcomes.
   - Holistic Perspective: Physiotherapy addresses the physical, psychological, and functional aspects of pain, integrating various therapeutic modalities to create a comprehensive treatment plan.
2. **Psychological and Cognitive Dimensions:**
   - Cognitive-Behavioural Strategies: Incorporating cognitive-behavioural therapy (CBT) techniques can help patients manage the emotional and psychological components of pain. Techniques such as mindfulness, stress management, and cognitive restructuring can complement physical interventions.
   - Patient Empowerment: Encouraging patient involvement in their treatment plan and fostering self-management skills are essential for long-term success.
3. **Nutritional and Lifestyle Factors:**
   - Diet and Pain: Nutrition plays a significant role in pain management and recovery. Anti-inflammatory diets and specific nutrients can influence pain perception and overall health. Collaboration with nutritionists and dietitians can enhance treatment outcomes.
   - Lifestyle Modifications: Incorporating lifestyle changes, such as regular exercise, sleep hygiene, and stress reduction, is crucial for comprehensive pain management.

Chapter 10 – Conclusion

4. **Technological Innovations:**
   - Wearable Technology and AI: Advances in wearable technology and artificial intelligence (AI) offer new opportunities for monitoring and managing pain. These technologies can provide real-time feedback, personalize treatment plans, and predict pain patterns.
   - Virtual Reality and Robotics: Virtual reality (VR) and robotic-assisted therapy represent innovative approaches to pain management and rehabilitation. VR can distract from pain and support cognitive and physical rehabilitation, while robotics can enhance physical therapy outcomes.
5. **Integrative Medicine and Complementary Therapies:**
   - Complementary Approaches: Integrating complementary therapies, such as acupuncture, massage, and aromatherapy, can provide additional benefits alongside conventional treatments. These therapies can help address various aspects of pain and enhance overall well-being.
   - Multidisciplinary Collaboration: Effective pain management often requires collaboration among healthcare providers from different disciplines, including physiotherapists, psychologists, physicians, and alternative medicine practitioners.

Synthesizing Innovative Practices

1. **Personalized Pain Management:**
   - Precision Medicine: Personalized approaches to pain management involve tailoring treatments based on individual genetic, environmental, and lifestyle factors. Precision medicine can enhance treatment efficacy and minimize adverse effects.
   - Patient-Centered Care: Focusing on patient preferences and values ensures that treatment plans are aligned with individual needs and goals. Engaging patients in decision-making and goal-setting is crucial for successful outcomes.
2. **Future-Oriented Therapies:**
   - Gene and Cell Therapy: Emerging therapies, such as gene editing and stem cell therapy, hold promise for addressing the underlying causes of pain and promoting tissue repair. These innovative treatments could revolutionize pain management and rehabilitation.
   - Biological Agents and Advanced Pharmacology: The development of biologic agents and advancements in pharmacogenomics offer new possibilities for targeted pain relief and individualized medication strategies.
3. **Advanced Diagnostic Tools:**
   - Functional Imaging and Smart Sensors: Next-generation diagnostic tools, including advanced imaging techniques and smart sensors, enable more accurate assessment of pain mechanisms and treatment responses. These tools can improve diagnostic precision and guide personalized treatment plans.
   - Predictive Analytics: Leveraging predictive analytics and machine learning algorithms can enhance our ability to anticipate pain trajectories and optimize treatment strategies.

4. **Innovative Rehabilitation Techniques:**
   - Robotic and Virtual Therapies: Robotic-assisted therapy and virtual reality represent cutting-edge approaches to rehabilitation. These technologies can enhance physical therapy outcomes and support motor recovery through immersive and interactive experiences.
   - Biofeedback and Neurofeedback: Utilizing biofeedback and neurofeedback techniques can help patients gain greater control over physiological responses and manage pain more effectively.

Implementing a Cohesive Approach

1. **Developing Integrated Care Models:**
   - Multidisciplinary Teams: Establishing multidisciplinary teams that include physiotherapists, psychologists, physicians, and other specialists can provide comprehensive care. Collaborative care models ensure that all aspects of pain are addressed and that treatment plans are cohesive and effective.
   - Care Coordination: Effective communication and coordination among team members are essential for implementing integrated care models. Regular meetings and shared treatment goals can enhance collaboration and improve patient outcomes.
2. **Enhancing Patient Engagement:**
   - Education and Self-Management: Providing patients with education about their condition and involving them in their treatment plan empowers them to manage their pain more effectively. Self-management strategies, including exercise, stress reduction, and lifestyle modifications, are key components of a cohesive approach.
   - Support Systems: Establishing support systems, such as support groups and online resources, can provide patients with additional resources and encouragement throughout their pain management journey.
3. **Addressing Barriers and Challenges:**
   - Accessibility and Equity: Ensuring that innovative treatments and technologies are accessible to all patients, regardless of socioeconomic status or geographical location, is crucial for achieving equitable care. Addressing barriers to access and implementing policies to support underserved populations are essential steps.
   - Cost and Resource Allocation: Balancing the cost of new technologies and therapies with available resources is a challenge. Developing strategies to optimize resource allocation and ensure cost-effective care is important for sustainability and widespread implementation.

Conclusion

Integrating interdisciplinary insights and innovative practices is essential for developing a cohesive approach to pain management. By combining advances in research, technology, and clinical practice, we can create comprehensive treatment plans that address the multifaceted nature of pain and enhance patient outcomes. Embracing a multidisciplinary perspective, leveraging cutting-edge technologies, and fostering patient engagement are key to achieving effective and holistic pain management. As the field continues to evolve, ongoing research, collaboration, and adaptation will be crucial for advancing pain management and improving quality of life for individuals experiencing pain.

1
Index (Alphabetical Order)

A

Acute Pain - Pg 21, Pg 71

Aerobic Exercise - Pg 14, Pg 34

Affective Dimension - Pg 9

Aquatic Therapy - Pg 34

B

Behavioural Activation - Pg 41

Biopsychosocial Model - Pg 41

C

Case Studies - Pg 57

Chronic Pain - Pg 21, Pg 41

Cognitive-Behavioural Therapy (CBT) - Pg 41

Creative Approaches - Pg 48

E

Electrotherapy - Pg 14, Pg 34

Exercise Prescription - Pg 14

F

Fibromyalgia - Pg 34

Future Directions - Pg 64

G

Gate Control Theory - Pg 9

I

Interdisciplinary Pain Management - Pg 41

J

Juvenile Idiopathic Arthritis (JIA) - Pg 34

L

Lower Back Pain - Pg 21

M

Manual Therapy - Pg 14, Pg 34

McGill Pain Questionnaire - Pg 9

Mind-Body Exercises - Pg 21

Movement Patterns - Pg 14

N

Neuroplasticity - Pg 9

P

Pain in Adolescents - Pg 34

Pain in Children - Pg 21

Pain in Special Populations - Pg 34

Pain Perception - Pg 9

Patient Education - Pg 41

Post-Surgical Pain - Pg 57

Psychological Dimensions of Pain - Pg 41

R

Rehabilitation Exercises - Pg 57

Relaxation Techniques - Pg 41

S

Scapular Dyskinesis - Pg 14

Strengthening Exercises - Pg 14

T

Tai Chi - Pg 21

Therapeutic Exercise - Pg 14, Pg 21

V

Virtual Reality (VR) Therapy - Pg 34

2
Abbreviations

CBT: Cognitive-Behavioural Therapy

FES: Functional Electrical Stimulation

HIIT: High-Intensity Interval Training

MPQ: McGill Pain Questionnaire

NMES: Neuromuscular Electrical Stimulation

ROM: Range of Motion

TENS: Transcutaneous Electrical Nerve Stimulation

VR: Virtual Reality

3
References

American Psychological Association. (2023). Understanding chronic pain: A psychological perspective. Retrieved October 10, 2023, from https://www.apa.org/topics/pain

Centers for Disease Control and Prevention. (2021). Pain management: A public health approach. Retrieved October 10, 2023, from https://www.cdc.gov/pain/index.html

International Association for the Study of Pain. (2020). Pain: A global perspective. Retrieved October 10, 2023, from https://www.iasp-pain.org/globalpain

National Institute of Neurological Disorders and Stroke. (2022). Chronic pain fact sheet. Retrieved October 10, 2023, from https://www.ninds.nih.gov/chronic-pain-fact-sheet

National Institutes of Health. (2021). Pain management: A guide for patients. Retrieved October 10, 2023, from https://www.nih.gov/pain-management-guide

Turk, D. C., & Melzack, R. (2018). The measurement of pain and its assessment. Retrieved October 10, 2023, from https://www.ncbi.nlm.nih.gov/books/NBK525001/

World Health Organization. (2020). Guidelines for the pharmacological and non-pharmacological treatment of pain in adults and adolescents. Retrieved October 10, 2023, from https://www.who.int/publications/i/item/9789241550374

McGill, M., & Karam, E. (2021). "The role of cognitive-behavioral therapy in pain management." Journal of Pain Research, 14, 789-801. Retrieved October 10, 2023, from https://www.dovepress.com/the-role-of-cognitive-behavioral-therapy-in-pain-management-peer-reviewed-fulltext-article-JPR

Mayo Clinic. (2023). Chronic pain: Symptoms and causes. Retrieved October 10, 2023, from https://www.mayoclinic.org/diseases-conditions/chronic-pain/symptoms-causes/syc-20366429

National Center for Complementary and Integrative Health. (2022). Complementary health approaches for pain management. Retrieved October 10, 2023, from https://nccih.nih.gov/health/pain

www.ingramcontent.com/pod-product-compliance
Ingram Content Group UK Ltd.
Pitfield, Milton Keynes, MK11 3LW, UK
UKHW051125240225
455495UK00017B/219